IMPROVE YOUR SELLING EFFECTIVENESS

A Practical Guide to Creative Selling

Stan Kossen

HarperCollins*CollegePublishers*

THE SELLING PROCESS

Maintaing Customer
Satisfaction

Closing
the Sale

Overcoming Sales
Resistance

Presenting and Demonstrating
the Sales Message

Approaching Prospective
Customers

Finding Qualified Customers
(Prospecting)

IMPROVE YOUR SELLING EFFECTIVENESS!
A PRACTICAL GUIDE TO CREATIVE SELLING

CONTENTS

Introduction to

IMPROVE YOUR
SELLING EFFECTIVENESS!

Who Can Benefit from this Guidebook?

Of course, it is difficult for any book to be all things to all people, and this book is no different. There are, however, three types of persons for whom this guidebook, *Improve Your Selling Effectiveness!,* can be highly beneficial:

- *The practitioner,* i.e., the person already involved in a professional selling position who wants to gain additional knowledge and skill in order to perform his or her tasks more effectively.

- *The career-minded,* i.e., the person who aspires to become a salesperson and wants to be eligible for a selling position when the opportunity arises.

- *The curious,* i.e., the person who is exploring the field of selling as a way of deciding whether he or she is really interested in becoming a salesperson one day.

What Is in this Guidebook?

Your guidebook, *Improve Your Selling Effectiveness*! is divided into 8 chapters as follows:

Chapter 1: The "Ologies" of Personal Selling

Chapter 2: Finding Qualified Customers

Chapter 3: Approaching Prospective Customers

What Should You Gain from this Guidebook?

One of the major purposes of your having obtained this guidebook is to improve yourself. What, then, should you be able to do if you put in a reasonable effort learning the concepts and techniques that you have studied? This guidebook, *Improve Your Selling Effectiveness!*, has some specific objectives, which are to enable you to:

- Utilize concepts borrowed from the behavioral sciences to gain a better understanding of the motives of buyers.

- Learn proven techniques for locating qualified customers.

- Create the favorable conditions that are important in approaching customers.

- Apply the major methods for gaining the attention of prospective customers.

- Apply the major characteristics of well–planned sales presentations.

- Utilize the proven techniques for delivering effective product demonstrations.

- Apply the major techniques for handling sales resistance to given sales situations.

- Understand the importance of active listening as a means for gaining customer interest and uncovering relevant information.

- Recognize the typical types of buying signals.

- Demonstrate the major techniques for closing sales.

- Describe the importance of post-closing activities.

- Understand the need for ethical behavior by salespeople.

- Identify some of the more common warning signs of deteriorating customer relations.

How Should You Use this Guidebook?

Read the learning objectives located at the beginning of each chapter. They help to provide you with a framework on which you can attach the information and knowledge that you acquire as you study the chapters.

Situated throughout each chapter are boxed inserts that raise questions related to materials located nearby. Take a break from your reading regularly, read the boxes, and see if you can answer the questions. Doing so will help to reinforce your newly–acquired knowledge and enable you to remember and apply the information for longer periods of time. Also, be certain to read the tables carefully since they typically contain important supplementary information related to the reading material.

At the end of each chapter is a list of terms that you should be familiar with after studying the chapter. Read each term, and then see if you can write down their meanings. A glossary can be found at the end of the text. The real judge of how well you've studied the material in each chapter is not your ability to *recognize* definitions when you reread the material but in how well you can *recall* information from your memory when you see the terms. The same concept applies to your answering the boxed questions.

This guidebook was written for you. The materials contained within have long been of assistance to professional salespeople who have utilized them. Learn and apply the information carefully. Doing so will help you to *improve your own selling effectiveness!*

Acknowledgments

Many people have contributed, either directly or indirectly, to this book. First, I would like to thank the master of all salespeople, my father, who spent his entire life in the selling field. I would also like to thank the sales managers with whom I worked for the many insights into selling that they provided me with. Their influence was immeasurable. Also of assistance were the students and participants in my classes and seminars who generously shared their real–world experiences with me.
Special appreciation is extended to the following professors of selling who provided me with helpful suggestions during the manuscript development phases of *Improve Your Selling Effectiveness!*

And finally, this book would not be complete without providing a round of kudos for my ever–helpful, always patient editors, Suzy Spivey, Jay O'Callaghan, and Anne Smith.

CHAPTER 1

THE "OLOGIES" OF PERSONAL SELLING

When you finish this chapter, you should be able to:

- List and describe six important factors that influence the buying behavior of consumers.

- Summarize the motivational theory of Maslow.

- Describe the effect of culture on consumer behavior. Describe the effect of attitudes on consumer behavior.

- Explain how social classes affect consumer behavior.

- Explain how perception affects consumer behavior.

- Describe how the purchase decision process affects consumer behavior.

- List the factors that tend to cause consumers to patronize a particular firm regularly.

- Cite the principal demand characteristics and buying motives of industrial purchasers.

CHAPTER 1

It is a universal truth that favorable consumer attitudes are prerequisites to marketing success.

Louis E. Boone

Have you selected the selling field as a career? Selling is an occupation that a small proportion of high school and college students actually intend to make their careers. Yet, more than 12 percent of the work force consists of people who have selected selling as their occupation.

There are two general areas of selling that you might enter: *retail* and *industrial.* When professional selling skills are employed, there are probably more similarities than differences between retail and industrial selling. You should select the sales area that best satisfies your own personal needs. Whichever you choose, your goals should include personal excellence and career satisfaction.

There are few occupations that are more challenging and demanding than selling. Working days are often long, there is often considerable job–related pressure, and travel away from home is frequently necessary. Disgruntled customers must be dealt with in an effective manner. Likewise, salespeople require a high degree of motivation and self–discipline.

In spite of these many challenges, however, salespeople tend to enjoy greater degrees of job satisfaction than persons in many other occupations. Salespeople often work in a relative free and non routine environment. Financial rewards can be substantial, often directly related to the salesperson's effort. Psychic rewards are also prevalent since salespeople can receive satisfaction from helping customers solve their problems and satisfy their needs.

3

THE "OLOGIES" OF SELLING—PSYCHOLOGY, SOCIOLOGY, AND CULTURAL ANTHROPOLOGY

Most of this textbook relates to what is referred to as the *selling process,* which primarily deals with the *how of selling techniques.* Learning about the selling process can provide you with information that can be used to develop and sharpen your selling skills. Equally important, however, is the *why of buying behavior,* that is, why individuals decide to buy a particular good or service.

To assist in understanding the why of buying behavior, the sales field has borrowed heavily from three behavioral science "ologies": *psychology, sociology,* and *social anthropology.* Psychology, for example, is concerned primarily with the scientific study of the behavior of individuals—why *people* behave as they do. Sociology emphasizes the scientific study of groups—why *groups* behave as they do. Social anthropology, a sub field of anthropology, is concerned with why *cultures* evolve and develop new customs, values, and attitudes.

Let's now take a look at the various causes of buying behavior.

THE CAUSES OF BUYING BEHAVIOR

No simple explanation tells us everything about why people buy products and services. Each person has a unique set of reasons for purchasing specific products. Your own motives for buying a particular product or service are likely to be quite different from another person's. Some individuals, for example, might want a product because of the feelings of *status or self–esteem* it provides. Others might want the same product because of specific *safety features.* And still others might desire the product because they believe it to be an *economically sound purchase.*

Wanted—Part–Time Selling Behavioral Scientists

Creative salespeople are, in a sense, part–time behavioral scientists. They should understand why consumers buy some goods and services and not others. Of course, since salespeople are not professional psychologists, sociologists, or social anthropologists, they should be cautious in applying incomplete knowledge. Nonetheless, as a salesperson, you should attempt to learn as much as possible about human behavior, especially the types of behavior that motivate consumers to purchase products. Now let's move into an examination of six important factors that tends to influence the buying behavior of consumers. They are:

- Needs and motives
- Culture
- Attitudes
- Social class
- Perception
- Purchase decision

THE NATURE OF NEEDS AND MOTIVES

Everybody has needs and wants that affect their buying decisions. When you already have something, then you don't really need it. When we refer to the term **need**, we'll mean the condition of *deprivation;* that is, the idea that *something is missing from a person's situation.* That "something" may be physiological (such as food), social (such as companionship), or psychological (such as self–esteem). The absence of food, for example, would tend to stimulate activity designed to satisfy that felt need: you would try to obtain some food. Stated differently, if you don't have something but you feel that you *must* have it, then you have a *need.*

Motives, too, are important to understand. A **motive** is a *feeling or condition that causes specific activity designed to bring about satisfaction.* The concept of motivation should become clearer as you progress through this chapter.

Primary Versus Secondary Needs

There are lots of things we could survive without, such as electricity, video camcorders, or cellular telephones, but we wouldn't survive for long without such basics as food, drink, adequate clothing, sleep, breathable air, and a satisfactory temperature; we *need* them. These are what psychologists call **primary needs**—that is, *basic* or *physical needs*.

We humans also have a variety of **secondary needs**—that is, *psychological* and *social* needs—which also tend to motivate or drive us. Our secondary needs are often *learned;* that is, we learn to need or want additional things, far less basic than food or drink. These secondary needs motivate us to act in certain ways. Among these needs are the desire to feel secure, to be with other people, to have sex appeal, to be respected as human beings, and sometimes even to climb mountains, bungee dive, or to skydive from airplanes. Everybody has needs, but not everybody tries to satisfy them in precisely the same fashion.

Nor does everybody have precisely the same needs. Not everyone needs the same number of hours of sleep nightly nor the same quantity of food, for example. Likewise, needs exist in each individual in varying degrees. As a salesperson, you could miss the opportunity to make a sale if you tried to appeal to needs or motives that your prospects don't even have.

Felt Needs Motivate

Some students of selling feel that salespeople don't actually sell; instead, they merely activate the wants and motives that already exist within the prospect. The primary focus, it is sometimes argued, should be on *buying* rather than *selling* since a person is not likely to purchase a product unless he or she *recognizes a need or want for it.* The salesperson, therefore, should attempt to uncover a need that may already exist since a need by itself will not necessarily motivate a person to act. The need must be *felt.* For example, assume you've discovered that the Senior Surgical Supply Company, one of your prospective customers, could save as much as $500,000 a year on office expenses if it were to adopt a system developed by your firm. In a sense, in order to save the $500,000, Senior Surgical *needs* your product.

6

What must occur before a need is likely to motivate a prospective customer to purchase a product?

When you haven't eaten for some time, hunger pangs usually help you recognize the need for food by creating a certain degree of inner tension. This tension then motivates you to act. Your action accomplishes a goal (the elimination of your hunger pangs) and thus relieves your tension. The achievement of your goal leads to a feeling of satisfaction, at least until the next time tension arises (see Figure 1.1). Now you should be able to see how salespeople are in the position to assist customers in recognizing needs, relieving tensions, and achieving goals.

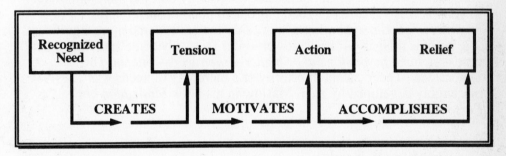

Figure 1.1 Recognized needs result in tensions and action designed to bring relief.

Satisfied Needs No Longer Motivate

As a person's basic needs become satisfied, the secondary or higher–order needs become increasingly more significant. For example, you must eat to live. If you are ravenously hungry, your first morsel of food might give you tremendous satisfaction. As you continue to eat, however, you may begin to experience what economists often refer to as "diminishing marginal satisfaction" from each additional portion of food. After a certain point (which varies with the individual) you discover that your basic need to satisfy your hunger drive has been met.

If you are extremely hungry *and* extremely tired, one of your drives or motives might be stronger than the other. For example, assume that you have not eaten or slept for 2 1/2 days and someone leads you into a comfortable room. As you enter, you see on one side of the room a perfectly baked, golden brown Cornish game hen, stuffed with wild rice speckled with slivered almond chips and accompanied by your favorite beverage. On the other side of the room you see a comfortable looking queen–sized bed. Which of the two intense drives will you satisfy first? You would probably favor your hunger drive. After satisfying yourself with a meal, you would probably find that the bed had begun to look increasingly inviting.

If you satisfy your basic needs, that is, acquire most of the food and adequate shelter you desire, other motives usually become more important to you. Perhaps *security* (a good retirement plan) or *social approval* (a home in a "good neighborhood"), or other factors become more significant. The point is this: as our basic, lower–order factors become satisfied, other needs—termed *psychological or higher–order* needs—increase in importance. This concept of priority or a hierarchy of needs was thoroughly developed by A.H. Maslow in his book *Motivation and Personality*.[1]

The Priority of Needs

Maslow suggested that human needs can be categorized into an *order of priority* (or a **hierarchy of needs**) and that each level of needs has to be satisfied to some extent before the next level assumes importance. Maslow developed a concept that distinguished five levels of human needs (see Figure 1.2) ranging from *basic, lower–order needs to psychological, higher–order needs:*

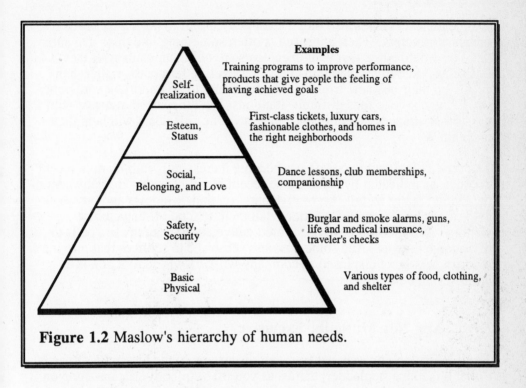

Figure 1.2 Maslow's hierarchy of human needs.

A cardinal point of the hierarchy–of–needs theory is that a *satisfied need ceases to motivate.* Lower–order needs don't become unimportant to a person, but higher–order needs achieve greater significance as basic needs are satisfied.

Why does a satisfied need cease to motivate?

Take, for example, a manufacturer whose sales representatives sell thermostatic control devices for heating systems. The need for a satisfactory temperature is basic, but the salespeople might try to appeal to the psychological or high–order needs of company executives by appealing to their desire for *self–esteem.* Executives are accustomed to controlling organizational situations. They might also prefer to control the temperature of their own offices rather than have it controlled from a central location.

9

Airline representatives also might attempt to appeal to the higher needs of business travelers. Their approach is often something like this: "I'm sure that you would agree that your executives are of higher caliber. If they *are* first–class executives, shouldn't they be traveling first class, rather than coach, on their business trips? If they are flying to an important conference where they have to face difficult situations, don't they need to arrive with the self–assurance and confidence that traveling first–class will help them maintain?"

The need to feel secure or safe has become increasingly important in recent decades, as indicated by some of the recent buying trends. Homeowners in the United States install "decorative bars" on their windows and buy guns and expensive electronic detection equipment to fend off unwelcome visitors. Automobiles have been fitted with electronic sirens and bells to discourage thieves. And some business subscribe to services that provide security personnel disguised as company workers whose function is to observe other employees.

Needs Are Not Mutually Exclusive

The implication you may get from our discussion of the hierarchy of needs is that it is like a stepladder; that is, as you lift your body past one rung on the ladder of needs, you are finished with it. *Not true!* Needs aren't mutually exclusive. For example, assume that you sell real estate to retired people in communities designed especially for them. The need for shelter— a house—is basic. But remember that people have higher–order needs as well. A retired couple may also have a *social need,* the desire for companionship with others of similar age and interests. Both types of needs may be important to them.

CULTURE AND CONSUMER BEHAVIOR

Someone once said, "We are what we eat"—and, in a sense, we all "eat" our environment. That is, we absorb mentally the various things we see and experience. This environment that we absorb is called culture. The term **culture** refers to the many environmental influences handed down from one generation to another that become a part of our present environment. Culture has a significant influence on what we see and do in a given situation. It also has a great influence on our needs and wants. For example, children who are raised in households where books and paintings are a normal part of the cultural environment are more likely to purchase such items for their own households.

How do cultural values affect the purchases of consumers?

Culture does not include those things we do instinctively, such as eating and sleeping. However, culture does influence how we satisfy those instincts. For example, some families satisfy their hunger instincts by eating squid, snails, tripe, or even cow tongue. Other families, based on their cultural backgrounds, appear nauseated at the mere mention of such foods. They may prefer to satisfy their hunger needs by eating "good old steak and potatoes."

Changing Cultural Influences

Cultural factors are continually in the state of flux. Changing cultural values and influences of all types are highly important to marketers since they significantly affect what they can sell to consumers. Some of the most important changes in cultural factors and value systems in recent years include:

- Evolving attitudes toward more equal roles at home and on the job

- More conservative sexual attitudes because of fear of sexually transmitted diseases

- Prevalence of a singles life–style

- Baby–boomers attaining middle–age Increased numbers of senior citizens

- Increased concern for security in older age

11

- Reduction in free spending habits and use of credit

- Changing ethnic composition of the United States

ATTITUDES AND CONSUMER BEHAVIOR

In addition to needs, motives, and culture, another factor that influences buying decisions is **attitude**, which, simply stated, is how a person feels about something. Attitudes relate to the beliefs and feelings people have and the ways they behave toward people, objects, and ideas. Let's now examine some factors that tend to shape consumer attitudes and also learn about some forces that could cause such attitudes to change. We will also see how we can put customer attitudes to use in selling.

Reference Groups

Our attitudes aren't inborn; they're typically learned from our families, friends, culture, and personal experiences. There are certain groups, therefore, that we tend to identify with for various reasons. These groups are termed **reference groups** and are likely to have a significant effect in shaping our tastes, values, and attitudes toward a host of things, such as for whom to vote in an upcoming election or what brand of denims or walking shoes to wear to school.

There are various types of reference groups. A **participational reference group** is one that individuals are integral members of, such as their families, clusters of friends, and their neighbors. A person's buying habits are often derived from these reference groups.

Does an individual have to be a member of a particular group to have his or her attitudes influenced by that group? Not necessarily. A group that an individual is not member of but would like to belong to is termed an **aspirational reference group**. For example, you might identify with a particular athletic team yet live thousands of miles from its home field. Many Ralders' football fans from the Oakland–San Francisco Bay Area continued to feel that the team was still theirs long after it moved from

12

Oakland to Los Angeles. In other situations, there are individuals who may not be wealthy yet they identify with "the rich and the famous" and, as a result, tend to copy some of their buying habits.

Many producers are well aware of the commercial value of reference groups. Some apparel manufacturers, for example, have provided at no cost to Olympic athletes all of the sports garb they needed to compete in the games. The generous manufacturers hoped to extract economic gain from the publicity value of the gifts since people who identify with the athletes, it is believed, tend to purchase the clothing lines of the donating manufacturers.

Reference may not always be to a group; it can also be to an individual. For example, some individuals might be influenced to purchase a particular brand of toothpaste promoted by a famous movie star.

How do reference groups affect the attitudes of consumers?

People are also influenced by **negative reference groups**. These are groups that a person doesn't want to identify with; therefore the person adopts attitudes *opposite* to those of the group. For example, why might some individuals choose to purchase a Honda motorcycle rather than a Harley–Davidson, or vice versa?

What Causes Attitudes to Change?

Since consumer attitudes are so significant to buying decisions, a major problem for salespeople is to determine how they can influence existing attitudes so that individuals are more favorably disposed to purchase their products. Most psychologists feel that attitudes tend to be highly resistant to change; consequently, In some cases, products or services have to be tailored to fit the attitudes of the consumer, while in other cases consumer attitudes themselves may be changed.

A Significant Experience. What are some things that just might change consumer attitudes? For one thing, a *significant experience* can influence a person's present attitudes. Assume, for example, that Jesse Steinberg never felt that helmets for motorcycle users were of much value, in spite of a law

13

requiring their use, and therefore refused to wear one. Let's also assume Jesse has a serious motorcycle accident and suffers severe head injuries.

Jesse is informed that wearing a helmet would have substantially lessened the extent of his injuries. After that, might he not change his attitude toward helmets?

Here's another example related to a significant experience: Cynthia Cynique has always pooh-poohed some of the rapid changes in computer technology, believing that many of the "new and different" innovations were more marketing gimmicks than real improvements in quality. She currently feels satisfied with her existing laptop computer that has 640 bytes of RAM and two 120k byte 3.5" floppy disk drives, with an adjustable super-twist LCD display. She uses her computer for both school work and in running a small part-time business.

A friend of Cynthia, Jason Johnson, invited her over for tea one day and showed her his new computer laptop, containing an 80486 microprocessor, 8 MB of RAM, a 80 MB hard disk drive plus a 3.5" 1.4 MB floppy disk drive, a backlit LCD display, plus a built-in fax/modem that enables faxes to be sent and received without printing out hard copies. Jason's computer came "bundled" with a windows environment, a spreadsheet, a word processor that provides desktop publishing quality plus outstanding or built-in graphics.

Cynthia tried out Jason's computer and couldn't believe her eyes! The computer was so fast and user friendly and could perform operations that she didn't even realize were possible. That "significant experience" changed her attitude. She rushed out the next day to the nearest computer store, "Terra Computers," and plunked down $2100 for a laptop just like Jason's. Can you think of any other significant experiences that could change a potential customer's mind?

Expectations. A person's *expectations* can modify attitudes, too. Let's return once more to our own friend, Jesse, and his helmet. Jesse might change his mind toward helmets if he believed and *expected* that he would receive a $250 traffic ticket from a law enforcement officer if caught without one on. Our other friend, Cynthia, also had expectations that modified her

14

attitudes. She *expected* to be able to accomplish more with less effort through the purchase of a more up–to–date laptop computer.

Recognition of a Want. *Recognition of a want* can also change attitudes. Let's assume that our same friend Jesse detests wearing neckties. In fact, he once exclaimed, "I'm my own man. I won't wear a necktie for anybody!" He might change his attitude, however, and be willing to wear a necktie if doing so were a precondition to getting a particular job that he strongly wanted.

A Shift in Self–Concept. Another factor that can alter a person's attitudes is a *shift in one's self–concept.* We all possess what is termed a **self–concept** or **self–image**, which means the way we see ourselves and the way we believe others feel about us. A distinction is sometimes made between the *actual self-concept* (the way we *really* see ourselves) and the *ideal self–concept* (the way we *want* to be seen or *would like* to view ourselves). A customer's purchases can be influenced by either. Assume, for example, that a person named Bernice Bayer is separated and in the process of being divorced from her husband, Barry.

During her marriage, Bernice's **actual self** influenced her into developing relatively conservative tastes: she drove a maroon four–door hatchback automobile and wore dark, somewhat old–fashioned clothes. After her separation, something happened to Bernice's self–concept. Her **ideal self** became dominant. She became an eligible woman who wanted to make a favorable impression on potential companions of the opposite sex. She recently purchased a handsome red luxury convertible automobile and some fashionable clothes, since these reflect the way in which she would *like* to be viewed by others—her ideal self. The way in which people perceive themselves, therefore, significantly influences their buying decisions.

How does a person's actual self differ from his or her ideal self?

Changes in a Product or service. *Changes in a product or in the quality of a service* can also change attitudes toward a product or company. A change in a product design, for example, can change a person's attitude

15

toward it. Or, a customer of an automobile repair shop may stop having her car serviced there because of a feeling that the service deteriorated when a new shop supervisor was hired.

Although attitudes tend to resist change what are some factors that could possibly alter a person's attitudes?

Putting Customer Attitudes to Use

Attitudes can be significant clues to how a salesperson should approach a particular prospect. Let's assume that one of your customers, Mrs. Blanche White, is known to prefer conservative clothes. She probably could be approached more easily if you also displayed conservative tastes when you called on her. If Mrs. White has political attitudes significantly different from yours, you would also be wise to avoid discussing politics in her presence.

You can often learn a lot about the personal attitudes of prospective customers by listening carefully to what they say about others. There is a fairly common tendency to attribute to others some of our own values and motives, a characteristic called **projection**. A Dutch philosopher, Spinoza, seemed well aware of this concept when he said, "When Peter talks about Paul, we often learn more about Peter that we do about Paul."

For example, you might ask your prospect—let's call him Leroy Carter–whether he is aware of a new system that your company recently installed for another company, the Ajax Sunburst Corporation. Carter might respond with something like: "No, but I'm not surprised. Ajax is quite a progressive firm. They always seem to be a giant step ahead of their competition."

From such a statement you might infer that Carter's attitude toward your products is quite favorable and that he could be a likely prospect for a purchase.

16

SOCIAL CLASS AND CONSUMER BEHAVIOR

Does a social class system exist in the United States? As much as some Americans prefer to feel otherwise, sociologists generally contend that such a system does exist, although not as predominantly as in some societies in the world. A **social class** is a group of people who have similar status In society. Their status, as perceived by the others in the community, is generally determined by their attained *educational level, occupation,* and by *where they live.* Surprisingly, income is not considered a primary determiner of social class, although it certainly can have a significant influence on a person's ability to maintain a particular social standing. Table 1.1 summarizes the principal categories of social class in the United States.[2]

Table 1.1 Principal social classes in the United States.

- *Upper class,* about 1 to 2 percent of the population, consisting of (1) established wealthy "old–money" families with inherited wealth *(upper–upper)* and (2) "new rich," owners of large businesses, certain professionals, and corporate executives *(lower–upper).* They tend to avoid mass merchandising, rather preferring exclusive types of goods and services. "Old–money" families tend to be less conspicuous in their consumption than the "new rich" and the upper–middle class.

- *Upper–middle Glass,* about 11 to 14 percent of the population, consisting of moderately successful business owners and professionals. Purchases by this group tend to conspicuously reflect their successes. They tend to purchase quality products and be concerned about their own and their children's future.

- *Lower–middle class,* about one third of the population, consisting of white–collar workers, small business owners, office workers. teachers, and technicians. This group is composed primarily of what is popularly considered "mainstream America," with traditional, conforming, and highly religious values. They tend to be more future oriented than the upper–lower class described below.

(Table 1.1 continued)

- *Upper–lower class,* about 38 percent of the population, consisting of skilled and semiskilled workers, service employees, and factory production workers. They tend to be security minded, earn fairly good incomes, and live more for the present than do the lower–middle class mentioned above.

- *Lower–lower class,* about 16 percent of the population, consisting primarily of unskilled laborers, chronically unemployed persons, certain ethnic immigrants, and long–term welfare recipients. They tend to make purchases that are necessities and that help them enjoy the present, rather than the future.

Class is not perceived by marketers as something either "good" or "bad," "better" or "worse," but rather as another method of segmenting markets. Marketers believe that the class with which individuals identify tends to influence their purchases far more than their level of income. The various classes frequently shop at different stores and purchase different types of automobiles even when their incomes are comparable to each other's.

Various studies indicate that social class has a significant influence over consumer behavior as a result of differences in three major areas.[3]

- *Sources of information.* Higher social classes tend to read different magazines and newspapers than those in the lower social classes, the former preferring publications that emphasize current events rather than those that dramatize romance and gossip, which tend to be preferred by the lower social classes. Similar patterns hold true for television watching–the higher social classes tend to prefer current event programs and drama, the lower social classes tend to prefer sitcoms, quiz shows, and "soaps."

18

- *Shopping patterns.* Many marketers attempt to cater to the different shopping patterns of the various classes. Some retailers, such as the Seattle–based chain of Nordstrom's stores, stress quality, snob appeal, and service in their sales promotions and advertising as a means of appealing to higher social class values. Other retailers, such as Gemco, attempt to appeal to a mass market of lower–class (lower–middle and upper-lower) values by stressing price and value, rather than snob appeal, in their advertising and promotion efforts.

- *Leisure activities.* In general, members of the different classes tend to select different leisure activities. For example, the higher social classes tend to prefer their own facilities, such as private golf, swim, and tennis clubs, whereas members of the lower–middle class tend to be the greatest users of public recreational facilities. Although the major sports of football, baseball, and basketball appear to be enjoyed by all social classes, certain activities—such as boxing, bingo, bowling, and wrestling—tend to be favored more by the lower classes.

How does the concept of social class relate to consumer purchases?

PERCEPTION AND CONSUMER BEHAVIOR

Salespeople should attempt to develop a sound understanding of the nature of perception, since what people see significantly influences their actions–whether they are in the process of selling or buying. Needs must be felt (perceived) before they motivate a person to act. And until a person feels (perceives) a need, he or she is unlikely to be moved to purchase a particular product.

Determinants of Perception

We've been using the term **perception**. Actually, what does it mean? *Perception* can be defined as *the way a person interprets a particular object, person, or situation.* We've already seen how *culture* can influence what we see and do in a given situation. The way we perceive is a fairly

19

complicated process and can be influenced by a wide variety of factors. Our discussion in this section will be restricted to three important influences on perception, which are:

- Snap judgments
- Selective perception
- Peer pressures

A brief discussion of each influence follows.

SNAP JUDGMENTS

Some people proudly believe that they can "size up a person right away." Unfortunately, their perceptions are often wrong. Many prospects (and salespeople) are guilty of making **snap judgments** before they have enough facts to come to valid conclusions. For example, they may feel certain that "your company doesn't provide adequate service," a belief that may be unfounded and based solely on a snap judgment. You should recognize that some prospects will make up their minds about you, your company, or its products with little factual evidence. And you may have to persuade them that your situation is different from the way they perceive it. And remember that you, too, might see your customers differently once you get to know them.

Selective Perception

You can expect to have to face numerous challenges as a salesperson, especially related to your attempts to overcome perceptual barriers. For example, there's the tendency for people (customers *and* salespeople) to see or hear what they want or are set to see and hear, and tune out any information that doesn't fit into their perceptual scheme. When people do this, they are engaging in what is termed **selective perception**. The following is an amusing illustration of this concept:

20

A lady went up to a famous painter and said: "Mr. Aggigoni, will you paint me in the nude? I will pay any fee you wish."

The painter thought for a while and then said: "Very well—but only if I can keep my socks on. Otherwise I shall have nowhere to put my brushes."

Here's a selling application of selective perception: Let's assume that you've just explained to a potential customer that although the price of your product is somewhat higher than the prices of your competitors, your product actually costs less to operate. You also explained that these savings, therefore, result in lower costs and higher profits for the customer over time. However, your prospect may "selectively perceive"—that is, focus only on the higher-cost portion of your message—and completely fail to hear what you said about higher profits. It is frequently important for you to get feedback from the customer in order to make certain that your message has been perceived as you intended it to be.

Peer Pressures

Related to cultural influences is the effect that our associates have on what we see, think, and do, often referred to as the **peer effect**. Our perceptions and attitudes are often much different when we are in the company of others from what they are when we're alone.

Some years ago, Solomon Asch conducted some experiments that helped to illustrate the apparent need people have to conform to the thinking of others.[4] Asch assembled several groups of eight people to participate in the experiments. The eight people sat around a table and were asked to judge the comparative lengths of various lines. Asch was sort of tricky, however. Only one person in each group of eight was a true subject; the others had been told in advance by Asch to conspire against that one by giving the *wrong* answers in a confident manner two–thirds of the time.

The guinea pigs (the one innocent victim in each group) were always the last to make their choices. Almost 40 percent of the time, these people went along with the incorrect decision of the group, admittedly because they didn't want to look silly in front of the others and not because they truly believed the group's answers. The **Asch conformity studies** clearly brought out the effect of group pressure on the perceptions and attitudes of individual members of a group.

The peer effect can also work in selling. Assume that two salespeople, Jill and Hal, are interviewing one prospect, whom we'll call Ms. Fonce. They are involved with what is sometimes referred to as **team selling**. Jill, one of the two salespeople, speaks to her counterpart: "Hal, wouldn't you also agree that Ms. Fonce could really benefit from acquiring out model XLZ–102?" Hal responds, "There's no doubt in my mind, Jill. Ms. Fonce, how do you feel about it?" As brought out by the Asch conformity studies, there could be a human tendency for Ms. Fonce to want to go along with the group—the two salespeople. Inherent in the team approach, however, is the potential danger of appearing to "gang up" on the prospect. Selling teams should avoid such an appearance.

How does the activity of *team selling* relate to consumer purchases?

THE PURCHASE DECISION PROCESS AND CONSUMER BEHAVIOR

How do your customers go about making buying decisions? Marketers believe that the typical person goes through a series of five stages when trying to decide whether to make a purchase. These activities are considered more as a process than as individual steps and are termed the purchase decision process. The common stages that most purchasers are believed to go through in the purchase decision process are listed in Table 1.2.

Table 1.2 The Purchase decision process

- Stage 1—Recognition of a need or want

- Stage 2—Search for information

- Stage 3—Evaluating alternative choices

(Table 1.2 continued)

- Stage 4—Making a choice

- Stage 5—Evaluating the choice made

Let's now look briefly at each purchase decision stage.

Stage 1—Recognition of a Need or Want

Do you remember our discussion of needs and wants? As you should recall, an unsatisfied need or want tends to result in action designed to achieve relief or satisfaction. Let's now trace a typical example of the purchase process. Assume that a young man named Jeffrey has a strong desire to own a compact disc player. Many members of his reference group (his friends) already have players. However, Jeffrey also remembers that the tires on his automobile have 60,000 miles and are going to need replacing soon. He wonders if now is a wise time for him to buy the compact disc player or, instead, he should save the money for the tires. He must resolve this conflict before moving on to the next stage.

Stage 2—Search for Information

Jeffrey believes that he really wants an improved sound system like his friends have, but he needs some information about the various units available for purchase. He has already received certain information in the past from newspaper and magazine advertising. He asks his friends for their opinions on different players. He also drops by SOUNDS RIGHT, a nearby electronics store, where he picks up some brochures describing some of the better units.

23

Stage 3—Evaluating Alternative Decisions

The next stage in Jeffrey's purchase decision process involves evaluating some of his possible choices. One of the units enables him to select up to 16 songs with random–access programming from a remote control device for $300. However, for $100 more, he could obtain a player that allows him to select up to 64 songs, also with random–access programming, plus it has a 7–disc capacity. The lower–priced model houses only one disc at time.

Stage 4—Making a Choice

Now Jeffrey must make a choice, the next stage in the purchase decision process. Jeffrey discovered during his evaluation stage that he could obtain credit and finance either compact disc player, the lower–priced one at payments of $20 a month or the more expensive 7–disc player for $21 per month. "What the heck," says Jeffrey to himself. "We only go around once. I've been working hard lately. I deserve a treat now and then." He also believes that by financing the player, he still will be able to afford his needed tires. He opts for the $400 set.

Stage 5—Evaluating the Decision Made

Depending on the purchase, many buyers develop various feelings and attitudes after their purchase. They frequently question the wisdom of their decisions, especially those related to more expensive non routine purchases. Jeffrey is actually quite pleased with the quality of the sound he gets from his new compact disc player. But he also feels an emotion that psychologists call **cognitive dissonance**, which is a form of stress caused by his uncertainty as to whether he should have made the purchase at this time. He now has an additional fixed expense each month that he would rather be without. And, since making his purchase, he has also learned that to obtain the maximum benefit from his new player he should buy a new set of speakers. However, his friends seem to be favorably impresses with his unit, and so he gradually begins to be pleased with his decision once again.

For an Individual Buyer—It Depends

Every purchaser doesn't necessarily go through every stage each time he or she buys a specific product. Stages may be bypassed altogether in certain situations, such as in routine and repeat purchases. Repurchasing your favorite toothpaste, for example, involves fewer stages than buying an automobile. Some products, therefore, especially lower–priced ones that are routinely bought without a lot of analysis, are termed **low involvement products**. More expensive products—those that are infrequently purchased and require more information—are termed **high involvement products**. The application of the purchase decision process, therefore, really depends on how much consumer involvement exists, which is influenced by the type of product, how frequently it is purchased, how much information is needed about the product, its cost, the extent of risk involved in the buying decision, and the perception of the buyer.

What is the difference between *low involvement* and *high–involvement products?*

REASONS FOR CONSUMER LOYALTY

Up to this point we have been discussing why people buy particular products–some writers call these reasons **buying motives**. Another classification of motives—called **patronage motives**—is concerned with why people repeatedly and consistently buy from a particular company. This concept should be easier to understand if you think about why you patronize the same firm on a regular basis.

One somewhat general reason could be because of *past satisfaction* you have received from the firm. Students of learning theory point out that we tend to repeat experiences that please us. If we have had consistently favorable experiences with a particular store, for example, we are likely to return for more—nor unlike a child who has discovered the secret hiding place of the cookie jar.

There are a number of reasons related to past satisfaction that tend to cause consumers to patronize a firm regularly. Most sellers strive zealously for consumer loyalty. How might the factors cited in Table 1.3 positively influence buyers to return to the source of their original purchase?

DEMAND CHARACTERISTICS AND MOTIVES OF INDUSTRIAL PURCHASERS

Household consumers, as we've learned, purchase products for a variety of motives, some rational but many of them emotional or psychological in nature. Purchasers for businesses and institutions also buy for a variety of reasons, sometimes rational and sometimes emotional, but the underlying motive for them typically relates to the opportunity to gain greater profits.

Table 1.3 Patronage motives that influence buyers to return to the source of their original purchases.

- A convenient location

- Favorable attitudes and behavior of sales personnel

- A positive public image or reputation, including appearance

- The availability of service and credit

- The speed of service

- Price (high for snob appeal, competitive or low to appeal to economy motives)

- A variety of goods available

- An atmosphere that creates good feelings among those who deal with the organization

---

Different Market Traits

The traits of industrial markets vary considerably from those of consumer markets, and they significantly influence industrial buying motives. In general, six demand characteristics are unique to industrial markets:

- *Demand is often derived* from another source. For example, increased consumer demand for shoes would result in a **derived demand** for leather. Increased demand for automobiles would result in a derived demand for steel, glass, and other industrial products.

- *Demand is generally more cyclical* than in many consumer goods industries. The demand for industrial goods tends to fluctuate drastically and is strongly related to current inventory policies and buyer expectations. For example, when shortages or rapid price increases are anticipated, forward buying (stockpiling) of goods often take place. When expectations about future economic conditions are bleak, inventories are often allowed to be depleted and little effort is made to replenish them. Thus there is **cyclical demand.**

- *Purchasing habits tend to be more rational.* In general, industrial purchasers are professionals with **rational buying motives**. They tend to be well informed as to the cost, quality and availability of the products they purchase. Of course, some industrial purchasers, such as a firm's purchase of an elaborate telecommunications system it didn't really need, seem to be emotional or ego–related, but most are rational.

- *Greater* **market concentration** *exists* in the industrial goods market. In the consumer goods field, large numbers of buyers are widely dispersed geographically. By comparison, there are relatively few buyers of industrial goods, and they tend to be more geographically concentrated.

- **Multiple buying decisions** are more common among industrial purchasers. Many buying decisions today are made by more than one person; sometimes they're made by established and formal **buying committees**, which are ongoing, established groups whose function is to determine the best sources for their organizational purchases. More will be discussed on this topic in later chapters.

- **Custom production** is more common in industrial markets. Typically, a consumer good is manufactured, then put up for sale. Industrial goods, however, are quite often custom–produced. A set of specifications for a product are released by the potential customer and bids are tendered on the basis of these specifications. If a bidding firm is not awarded the contract, it does not manufacture the specific item.

And Just What Are Their Motives?

In general, industrial buyers are better informed and more rational than are average consumers. As a result, the more rational the sales appeal, the more likely industrial prospects are to buy. Businesses cannot function for long without profits, and the sensitive salesperson realizes that the *profit motive* is of paramount importance in the buying decisions of industrial and commercial purchasers. As a result, many sales appeals relate to the profit motive, as discussed briefly below. (See Table 1.4 for a list of the factors that influence buying decisions of industrial purchasers.)

Table 1.4 Factors that influence buying decisions of industrial purchasers.

• Price	• Flexibility
• Quality	• Fear
• Salability	• Emotions
• Prestige	

Price. *Price is* an important factor in the purchase of many industrial products. However, the cheapest product is not always the item that a purchaser wants. More important than its price are two other factors: how it contributes to the total cost of the product the manufacturer is producing and how it affects the total cost of operations. A higher–priced item can actually reduce the unit cost of production if it contributes toward greater efficiency in a firm's activities. Sometimes, for example, a purchaser will buy a product costing somewhat more than a comparable foreign–made product, but the certainty and dependability of the domestic supplier may be more important to the prospective purchaser than the initial price.

Why wouldn't a manufacturer necessarily purchase the cheapest or the highest quality of materials?

Quality. If you were an industrial buyer, how important would you consider the appeal of *quality?* Generally, quality has quite a significant appeal, but would you necessarily purchase a product of greater quality than you really needed? For example, If you were purchasing toilet tissue for employee rest rooms, would you buy the highest quality? Would your choice of tissue be different if you were a buyer for the Marriott hotel chain? If you were a manufacturer, would there be much logic in purchasing a component part that would considerably outlast a final product? Often, it's far more important for a product to be of a *consistent* and *uniform* quality than that it be of a particularly high quality.

Salability. Industrial and commercial buyers are also motivated by a products *salability,* a highly significant consideration. Assume that you are an industrial buyer. Try to think of an item you might purchase. Will it help you sell your own products? If not, will you be likely to buy it? Some purchased items can enhance salability while others might detract. Furthermore, a product that seems to improve salability during one period could be detrimental during a subsequent period if public attitudes or government legislation changed.

Fear. Another factor that motivates is *fear*. Although not a pleasant emotion, fear and the desire to feel more secure are strong motivating factors in the purchase of numerous industrial goods and services. The felt need for *protection* is a significant reason why such goods and services as safes, fire extinguishers, insurance policies, and patrol services are purchased.

Evidence of this desire for protection is apparent in the yellow pages of any typical telephone directory. "Guard dogs leased—24–hour radio dispatches" reads one. Established to meet today's demand for a NEW security in commerce, education, industry, and property management reads another.

Flexibility. The desire for *flexibility is* another motive in purchasing some products. An item that can be used for more than one operation is usually preferable to a less flexible one. For example, assume that a company is involved in international markets, and its managers travel to other countries regularly with their laptop computers. Since the computers need electricity for recharging their batteries, the managers might prefer to purchase computers that come with electric adapters that adjust automatically to different electric currents. (Electrical current is 110–115 volts in the United States and 220–240 volts in many other countries. A 220 electrical current would normally burn out an item that was designed for 110 volts.)

Emotions. Industrial purchasers are also human beings; they don't hang their *emotions* on hooks outside their offices. As a result, not all purchases are the result of rational decisions. A purchasing manager, for example, may simply like a particular salesperson and buy strictly on the basis of friendship. Some purchases may be made on a *reciprocity* basis in the belief that it is sound business practice for a firm to buy some products from its own customers. The practice of you scratch my back and I'll scratch yours,"—that is, reciprocity—could be an undesirable policy in certain instances, especially where a purchaser may not be obtaining the desired quality at a favorable price.

When might reciprocity be an undesirable business practice?

Prestige. Also, industrial purchasers sometimes ignore rational buying motives and buy a product, such as a particular make or model of automobile for company use, strictly because of the *prestige* it affords its users.

These are terms that you should now be familiar with:

- need
- motive
- primary needs
- secondary needs
- hierarchy of needs
- culture
- attitude
- reference groups
- participational reference group
- aspirational reference group
- negative reference groups
- self–concept (self image)
- actual self
- ideal self
- projection
- social class
- perception
- snap judgments

- selective perception
- peer effect
- Asch conformity studies
- team selling
- purchase decision process
- cognitive dissonance
- low involvement products
- high involvement products
- buying motives
- patronage motives
- derived demand
- cyclical demand
- rational buying motives
- market concentration
- multiple buying decisions
- buying committees
- custom production

NOTES

1. Abraham H. Maslow, *Motivation and Personality,* (New York: Harper & Row, 1954).

2. Adapted from Richard P. Coleman, The Continuing Significance of Social Class to Marketing, *Journal of Consumer Research,* December 1983, pp. 265–280; Dennis Gilbert and Joseph A. Kahl, The American Class Structure: A Synthesls, in *The American Class Structure: A New*

Synthesis (Homewood, IL: Richard D. Irwin, 1984); and Kotler and Armstrong, *Principles of Marketing,* 4th ed. (Englewood Cliffs, NJ: Prentice–Hall, 1989), p. 122.

3. As reported in William H. Cunningham, et al, *Marketing: A Managerial Approach* (Cincinnati: South–Western Publishing, 1981), pp. 165–166.

4. Solomon E. Asch, Effects of Group Pressure upon the Modification and Distortion of Judgments, in *Readings in Social Psychology,* edited by Eleanor E. Maccoby, Theodore M. Newcomb, and Eugene L. Harley (New York: Holt, Rinehart and Winston, 1958), pp. 114–183.

CHAPTER 2

FINDING QUALIFIED CUSTOMERS

When you finish this chapter you should be able to:

- Describe the importance of prospecting

- Know where to find prospects

- Apply the concepts for qualifying prospects

- Recognize the need for planning and keeping adequate records

CHAPTER 2

Remember, the thing that got you where you are today isn't necessarily going to keep you there.

Jack Wilner, Director of Training
Blue Bell Division of VF

Attached to the wall in the office of a small midwestern business establishment is a plaque bearing the inscribed words:

Ours is a nonprofit business—but it wasn't planned that way!

Few private business concerns plan to be nonprofit organizations; they can't exist for long without the regular inflow of revenues in excess of their expenses. Who is it that often has the key responsibility for generating such revenues? That's right! The salesperson. But the act of selling by itself is not enough; goods and services must be sold at a *profit*. In order to fulfill this responsibility, salespeople are expected to apply sound and proven concepts of selling to their activities.

In this and subsequent chapters, you will examine the **selling process**. Just what is the selling process? It can be defined as the *essential elements involved in the activity of personal selling*. It is presented in six steps (see Figure .2.1). You are going to learn about the first step in this chapter—*prospecting* for customers, including something called the *pre approach*. You will explore such topics as why prospecting is important, where you can find prospects, how you can determine if they are qualified to buy your products or services, and why you must plan and maintain adequate prospecting records if you want to be effective in pre approaching prospective customers.

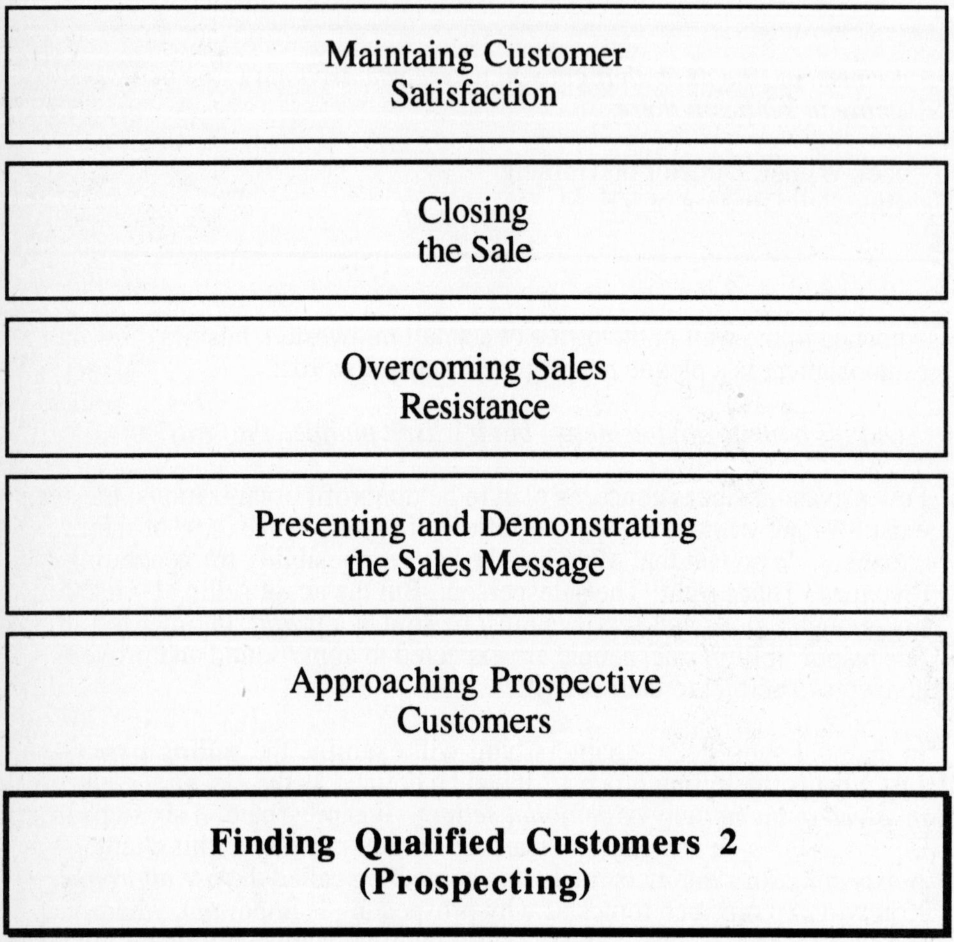

Maintaing Customer Satisfaction

Closing the Sale

Overcoming Sales Resistance

Presenting and Demonstrating the Sales Message

Approaching Prospective Customers

Finding Qualified Customers 2 (Prospecting)

Figure 2.1 The selling process is a series of activities with finding qualified prospects being the first.

WHY IS PROSPECTING IMPORTANT?

Have you ever heard that classic bit of advice, "Build a better mousetrap and the world will beat a path to your door ? Such a belief is not only unfounded today but was probably never true. If you were to build a better mousetrap without attempting to sell it, you would be more likely to observe untrampled grass growing knee-high on the narrow path in front of your doorstep.

Although sales personnel in retail stores must ordinarily wait for customers to come to them, sellers of many types of mousetraps must actively seek out prospective buyers. For example, tremendous competition exists among producers of computer work stations. Firms such as Sun Microsystems, Digital Equipment, Hewlett-Packard, and IBM seldom wait for customers to ask to purchase their products. Instead, their sales forces are continually searching for new customers. This exploration for new accounts is referred to as **prospecting**, which can be defined as *the step in the selling process that involves locating potential customers.*

What's the Difference Between a Prospect and a Suspect?

In order to avoid wasting considerable time, it's extremely important for you as a salesperson to sort out so-called *suspects* from *prospects*. **Suspects**, also called **leads**, are considered to be any person who might *possible* buy your products or services, but whom you've not yet placed into the prospect category. **Prospects** are what you hope your leads really are. These are individuals or organizations that can *benefit* from your product or service, can *qualify financially* to make a purchase, and have the *authority* to influence or make buying decisions.

Virtually all persons you might contact could be considered to be suspects before you've uncovered certain qualifying information about them, since there is always the possibility that they *might* buy you product. *Possibilities*, however are not *probabilities*--every suspect isn't necessarily a prospect.

To illustrate, assume that you intend to phone every person listed on page 143 of the local telephone directory. Will all of them purchase your product? It's *possible*, but is it *probable*? Your experience and wisdom should tell you that such an event is unlikely. You can waste considerable amounts of time if you assume that every breathing specimen of *Homo sapiens* is a hot prospect. On the other hand, you can also waste a disproportionate amount of time *overqualifying* prospects, that is, uncovering more information about potential buyers than you really need. In short, a prospect is a suspect who has a need or desire for your product. You, the salesperson, can assist the suspect who is unaware of his or her need for your product in becoming a prospect.

Explain in your own words the difference between a suspect and a prospect? Why is it important for you to understand the difference?

Telephone Directory		Boat Owner's Register	
Williams, A. 111-1111	Williams, Z. 999-9999	Jones, A. 292-2929	Jones, Z. 929-9292
Williams, B. 222-2222	Williams, Y. 888-8888	Jones, B. 333-3333	Jones, F. 444-4444
Williams, A. 111-1111	Williams, Z. 999-9999	Jones, A. 292-2929	Jones, Z. 929-9292
Williams, B. 222-2222	Williams, Y. 888-8888	Jones, B. 333-3333	Jones, F. 444-4444
Williams, A. 111-1111	Williams, Z. 999-9999	Jones, A. 292-2929	Jones, Z. 929-9292
Williams, B. 222-2222	Williams, Y. 888-8888	Jones, B. 333-3333	Jones, F. 444-4444
Williams, A. 111-1111	Williams, Z. 999-9999	Jones, A. 292-2929	Jones, Z. 929-9292
Williams, B. 222-2222	Williams, Y. 888-8888	Jones, B. 333-3333	Jones, F. 444-4444
Williams, A. 111-1111	Williams, Z. 999-9999	Jones, A. 292-2929	Jones, Z. 929-9292
Williams, B. 222-2222	Williams, Y. 888-8888	Jones, B. 333-3333	Jones, F. 444-4444
Williams, A. 111-1111	Williams, Z. 999-9999	Jones, A. 292-2929	Jones, Z. 929-9292
Williams, B. 222-2222	Williams, Y. 888-8888	Jones, B. 333-3333	Jones, F. 444-4444
Williams, A. 111-1111	Williams, Z. 999-9999	Jones, A. 292-2929	Jones, Z. 929-9292
Williams, B. 222-2222	Williams, Y. 888-8888	Jones, B. 333-3333	Jones, F. 444-4444
Williams, A. 111-1111	Williams, Z. 999-9999	Jones, A. 292-2929	Jones, Z. 929-9292
Williams, B. 222-2222	Williams, Y. 888-8888	Jones, B. 333-3333	Jones, F. 444-4444
Williams, A. 111-1111	Williams, Z. 999-9999	Jones, A. 292-2929	Jones, Z. 929-9292
Williams, B. 222-2222	Williams, Y. 888-8888	Jones, B. 333-3333	Jones, F. 444-4444
Williams, A. 111-1111	Williams, Z. 999-9999	Jones, A. 292-2929	Jones, Z. 929-9292
Williams, B. 222-2222	Williams, Y. 888-8888	Jones, B. 333-3333	Jones, F. 444-4444
Williams, A. 111-1111	Williams, Z. 999-9999	Jones, A. 292-2929	Jones, Z. 929-9292
Williams, B. 222-2222	Williams, Y. 888-8888	Jones, B. 333-3333	Jones, F. 444-4444

-143-   -55-

SUSPECTS   **PROSPECTS**

Figure 2.2 A list of registered boat owners would be a more likely source of prospect for boat insurance than would a general telephone directory.

Why Is Prospecting so Important?

During the normal pressures in a typical day in your life as a salesperson, you might find it difficult to allot time for prospecting. However, an understanding of why prospecting for new accounts is so essential may help to motivate you into it. You should become aware that prospecting is one of the most important responsibilities you have as a salesperson. Why? Because the volume of sales in a particular territory seldom remains constant; it either grows or diminishes. Without a consistent, planned prospecting program, the amount of business activity is likely to decline. Take a careful look at Table 2.1 to uncover some key reasons why sales volume tends to decline without a planned prospecting program.

41

Table 2.1 Reasons why sales volume tends to decline without a planned prospecting program.

- Some customers may stop doing business with your company.
- Some customers may relocate and move out of your sales territory.
- Some customers may go out of business due to bankruptcy.
- Some customers may go out of business due to death, illness, or accident.
- Some customers may "downsize" and lay off large numbers of employees.
- Some customers may merge with or be absorbed by larger firms that have their own well-established suppliers.
- Your purchasing contact with a particular firm may be promoted or transferred, may retire, or may resign.
- Your customer may switch from the use of purchasing agents to a buying committee, thus changing your usual pattern of selling.

Integrating prospecting with your other sales activities is a must if your sales production is to grow rather than stagnate.

How Do You Prepare for the Prospecting Activity?—the *Preapproach*

An activity that relates directly to prospecting is the **preapproach**. The preapproach is *an activity that involves your obtaining as much relevant information as necessary about prospects before contacting them personally.* In simple terms, the preapproach is the process of separating "prospects" from "suspects." Examine Table 2.2, which cites the principal types of questions that you as a salesperson should try to answer related to the preapproach process.

Table 2.2 Typical types of questions that a salesperson should attempt to answer during the preapproach.

- Who actually is the customer? (Include who will influence the buying decision and would be likely to use the product or service.) Do you know the correct spelling and pronunciation of their names?

- What does the customer need? (This information will aid you in developing a relevant sales presentation.)

- What other information could be useful in approaching the customer? (For *companies:* background information on the firms, their past results and current financial conditions, and their products and markets. For *individuals:* personal information including hobbies, interests, educational background, and involvement in the community.)

- When is the best time to call? (You should select a time when the prospect will be most receptive to your message.)

Uncovering answers to the questions in Table 2.2 can help you in four major ways:

- It provides relevant information and insight about potential customers to determine whether they qualify for purchase.

- It helps determine effective strategy for approaching prospective customers and preparing sales presentations just for them.

- It reduces the likelihood of making serious errors during sales presentations.

43

- It helps instill more confidence in the salesperson, since it involves prior planning for sales interviews.

An amusing story helps to illustrate the importance of developing a sound preapproach process:

> A salesperson telephoned a prospective customer and the phone was answered by what was obviously a young boy. "Is your mother or father home?" the salesperson asked. The child said no. Well, is there anyone else there I can speak to? asked the salesperson. "My sister, the youngster piped up. "Would you get her please?" requested the salesperson. There was a long silence, then the salesperson heard the little boy's voice again. I'm sorry, he said, but I can't lift her out of the playpen.

> *Explain the purpose of the preapproach. What are some of principal questions you should answer as a part of the preapproach process?*

WHERE ARE PROSPECTS LOCATED?

To be successful in achieving your sales goals, you must continually be on the alert for ways to maintain and increase your volume of business. To avoid wasting valuable time, you should have a *plan* for maintaining an effective and useful prospect list. Where do you locate names for your prospect record file? The answer varies, depending principally on the nature of the product or service you are selling. A life insurance salesperson, for example, would be unlikely to use a list of retired senior citizens as a source of leads. A sales representative for a steel manufacturing company would be unlikely to canvass a suburban neighborhood door to door looking for potential buyers of cold-rolled steel.

You should be careful not to scratch someone off your list or snub someone who might either become a prospect or refer you to one. Sometimes, for example, in addition to purchasing agents or managers, secretaries and assistants make significant buying decisions.
What are your principal sources of potential customers? Table 2.3 lists the main ones. Each is briefly discussed below.

44

Table 2.3 Principal sources of potential customers.

- Your own company

- Your present customers

- Former prospects

- Friends, acquaintances, and neighbors

- Other salespeople

- Junior salespeople and bird dogs

- Newspapers, directories, registers, and special lists

- Personal observation

- Cold canvas technique

- Blitz technique

- Trade fairs and exhibitions

- Clubs and social groups

- Group party plans

- Surveys

- Telephone and mail inquires

- Use of videocassettes and computer diskettes

FINDING QUALIFIED CUSTOMERS

Try your own company

Your own company can sometimes be a valuable source of prospective purchasers. Some firms, such as Hewlett-Packard, advertise their products in specialized and technical publications. As a result, prospective buyers often *write or telephone for product information,* which can then be provided personally by sales representatives. Some firms offer free gifts in their advertisements as an inducement; these can be presented to prospective customers, along with creative sales messages.

Service or repair personnel within your company can also be a profitable source of leads. A claims adjuster, for example, could give insurance agents the names of persons who, although insured with other companies, were pleased with the settlement of their particular claims. Or the service department of an auto dealership or office equipment company could be a source of names of individuals ready to replace their older equipment.

Try your present customers

Easily overlooked but often a lucrative source of leads are your past and present customers. For example, they may be about to deplete their supply of items previously purchased from you and thus be in need of restocking. Or they may have recently realized that they have, after all, a previously unrecognized need for one of your products.

You should also attempt to employ with your present customers what is termed the **endless–chain method**, a process that simply involves *asking your existing customers for the names of prospective ones.* This approach, as illustrated in Figure 2.3, can provide you with a virtually endless supply of potential customers.

46

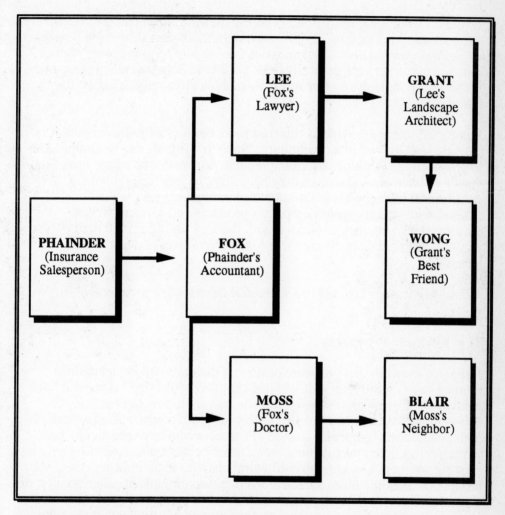

Figure 2.3 Endless–chain prospecting method for a hypothetical insurance salesperson named Pheinder.

A related technique, termed the **referral method**, goes one step beyond the endless-chain method. In the referral method, the salesperson *obtains not only names but also a personal note or letter of introduction.* Your satisfied customers are generally quite willing to help you along these lines. Some salespeople even offer rewards, such as gifts and discounts, for referred leads.

Some customers are what is referred to as **centers of influence**; that is, they are well known in a community. Such individuals can be another aid to prospecting. Assume, for example, that you have insured the life of the mayor of the town. She or he may be willing to provide you with a **testimonial letter**, which is a sales tool indicating that the customer is pleased with you and your company's products and service. When customers tell you they're pleased with the way you've served their accounts, don't hesitate to ask them for referred leads and testimonial letters.

How might you make use of testimonial letters when prospecting?

Try Former Prospects

Have you ever felt that you were positively disinterested in a particular product only to find later that you had changed your mind? If so, you have plenty of companions. As a salesperson you should recognize that, although individuals may not purchase your product when you first call on them, conditions frequently change. Prospects who have practically been written off as potential customers sometimes become dissatisfied with their existing sources. Occasionally structural changes in an industry cause your products to become more attractive from the standpoints of price, quality, or dependability. Or changing international currency values, newly imposed tariffs on imported goods, or shortages of competing products may make your products less costly than those of foreign sources.

Furthermore, over periods of time, your former prospects may become more aware of the advantages and uses of your products. Regardless of the reasons why former prospects change their minds, a creative salesperson recognizes that persistence in sales activities often pays off. You should be continually alert to any changes that might turn a former "suspect" into a full-fledged "prospect."

Try Your Friends, Acquaintances, and Neighbors

"I want all my customers to be my friends and all my friends to be my customers." As desirable a philosophy as this may appear, you should exercise caution when using friends as prospects. If you become pesty with your valued friends, you may discover that one day they are no longer friends. Some salespeople prefer not to do business with their friends, close social acquaintances, or neighbors, mainly because of unfavorable experiences with such contacts who expect special favors or discounts. Also some salespeople, almost unknowingly, develop the reputation of being the type who continue to push their wares every moment they are with friends or neighbors. Individuals whose friendship you value may begin to think when they see you, "Oh, oh, here comes that pushy sales one again." The following story helps to illustrate what can happen when you run out of friends!

A seven–year-old boy named Jason decided to sell garden seeds to buy a bicycle. One day Jason's good friend, Jessica, saw him and the following conversation ensued:

Jessica   How you doing with your seed sales, Jason?

Jason   Great! I'm a fantastic little salesperson! I sold one to my mom, to my uncle Harold, to my cousin Clyde, my aunt Fannie, my dad, my neighbor, my sis, and my brother–in–law.

Jessica   What's so great about that? If you're so good let's see you sell some seeds to a stranger.

Jason   But Jessica—I'm only a child. I don't know any strangers.

Moral: For some salespeople—when they run out of friends, they're in trouble.

49

Try Other Salespeople

An alert salesperson can obtain prospective customers from what might appear to be unlikely sources. For example, competing salespeople are occasionally generous with useful information and may unwittingly furnish you with leads or facts about a potential customer. Or a salesperson whose company doesn't produce a product you sell may generously volunteer the name of someone who could use your product. Always keep your eyes and ears tuned to sources of potential customers.

Try Spotters and Sales Associates

Some firms employ people new to selling as **spotters**, whose job is to try to locate leads for more experienced salespeople. This approach enables more seasoned sales personnel to spend more of their time in actual selling.

A similar approach uses **sales associates**, who are located by the salesperson rather than the company. Sales associates, are typically individuals who have regular jobs with other companies but are in the position to discover leads for the salesperson. For example, an employee of a boat supply company could provide leads to a person selling boat owner's insurance. The sales associate is paid by the salesperson on the basis of successfully completed sales.

What is the major distinction between a spotter and a sales associate. How do you feel about their use?

Try Newspapers, Directories, Registers, and Special Lists

A creative salesperson, continually struggling to find new customers, should take full advantage of the numerous prospecting opportunities that arise. These include an often overlooked but frequently rewarding source of prospects: *public information,* which is readily available to anyone interested. The potentially useful sources are listed in Table 2.4:

50

Table 2.4 Principal sources of potential customers.

- *Current items in newspapers* (such as the opening of new retail stores or a change of ownership in established ones).

- *New construction applications* (contractors may be prospects for your products or services).

- *License applications* (such as business permits, boat and automobile registrations).

- *Lists of recorded warranties* (these can indicate when individuals will be ready to replace their aging products).

- *Voter registration lists* (these can be obtained from precinct captains). *Professionally prepared lists* sold by list brokers (these include lists of subscribers of publications in all fields—boating, hiking, fishing. computing, and so on).

- *Lists kept by those whom you patronize* (such as your insurance agent, garage repair person, or banker).

- *Telephone directories* (including the white and yellow pages)

Try to observe

Salespeople are continually "on the go." Creative salespeople, no matter what they're doing, are continually sensitive to potential sources of prospects. Sometimes a casual remark by an acquaintance or an item in a newspaper can alert the salesperson with a "nose for prospects." Some sales people develop a keen sense for spotting potential customers in virtually any situation.

51

Here's a related anecdote:

Two shoe salespeople visit a lesser-developed country. One cabled his office, "No prospect for sales; nobody wears shoes here." The other salesperson cabled, "Send stock immediately; inhabitants barefoot, desperately need shoes."

Try Cold Canvassing

Another method for finding prospects, termed the **cold canvass technique**, attempts to utilize the law of averages. Assuming that you have reasonable sales abilities and a useful product, then—based on the cold canvass approach—you are likely to sell a certain percentage of all those contacted; that is, the law of averages should work for you.

Prospects are not preselected for the cold canvass approach. Instead, you choose a specific group and then attempt to contact as many individuals in the group as possible. For example, as a fax machine salesperson, you might call on every office in a particular building. Since you will typically know little in advance about your "suspects," you will have to attempt to qualify them and uncover their needs during your initial presentation.

You should consider utilizing the approach followed by many professional salespeople who set aside a specific time to cold canvass for prospects. For example, you could plan to devote every other Thursday *exclusively* to the activity of making **cold calls**, that is, calling on prospects whom you've never contacted before. Planned prospecting days, such as these, help to eliminate the problem of procrastinating the all-important activity of prospecting for new accounts.

How might the cold canvass approach to prospecting consume more time than alternative prospecting techniques?

Far too frequently, a salesperson's efforts at prospecting go little beyond making the statement, One of these days I've got to do some cold canvassing for new prospects." These words are analogous to statements like, "One of these days I'm going to start doing some stomach exercises." Often those days never come without following through with a specific plan. The cold canvass approach is difficult and requires a substantial amount of self-discipline, but it can be used with success by the persistent and patient salesperson.

Try the Blitz Technique

A modification of the cold canvass approach is called the **blitz technique**. Its purpose is to saturate a particular region in as short a time as possible. For example, a team of sales representatives may be temporarily assigned to a particular territory to try to expand the number of outlets for their products. They might call on every retail store in a specific town, hoping to develop leads that they will then turn over to regular company salespeople in that territory for follow–up.

What is the principal advantage of the blitz technique of prospecting?

Try Trade Fairs and Exhibitions

Some firms display their wares at **trade fairs** and **exhibitions**. Periodically presented in major cities are such events as boat shows, electronic equipment shows, computer fairs, and furniture shows, where product literature is distributed and products are described to visitors. Names of interested individuals are often obtained and given to company salespeople for follow-up purposes.

Try Clubs and Social Groups

For some products or services, clubs as well as **civic and social groups** can also be sources of prospective customers. Even if you are not a member of a particular group, you may know or meet someone who is a member and who could provide you with a list of prospective customers. Attending the meetings of such groups can also sometimes result in new leads. There is an ever-present danger, however, of your overextending your available time if you become too deeply involved in civic groups and clubs. Some salespeople have discovered, to their dismay, that they became active to the detriment of their jobs and families.

Try Group Party Plans

Some types of products—such as cookery, household cleaning agents, and cosmetics—lend themselves to being sold at **party groups**. These typically are gatherings at the home of a volunteer host who is responsible for inviting friends and acquaintances—potential customers for the demonstrated products. A significant advantage of group party selling is the opportunity for the salesperson to concentrate a relatively large number of prospects in one location.

Try Surveys

Surveys are another technique used to locate prospective buyers. This approach uses questionnaires to uncover potential needs of customers and thus pave the way for specific sales presentations. Unfortunately, the unscrupulous use of surveys by some salespeople have created skeptical attitudes toward them.

Try Telemarketing

Calling on prospects in person is an expensive activity, often involving transportation and parking costs plus considerable travel time. **Telemarketing** is a prospecting technique that has become quite popular as a way of reducing selling costs. Telemarketing is actually a broad set of activities that involves the use of the telephone to support and, at times, to serve as a substitute for personal face-to-face selling. It is frequently used in prospecting activities.

Prospecting with the use of the telephone often results from **telephone and mail inquiries** by prospective customers. A considerable amount of advertising today urges readers to obtain additional product information either by telephoning a toll-free number or by mailing a cut-out coupon or postage-free card. As a means of encouraging greater response, the readers are sometimes offered a free gift or brochure.

Telephone and mail inquiries are typically analyzed and screened for their usefulness as potential prospects and then turned over to local company salespeople for follow-up with a sales presentation. (Table 2.5 provides a list of suggestions for effective telephone use when talking with prospective or existing customers.)

Table 2.5 Guidelines for effective telephone use.

- Don't be sneaky; always **identify** yourself, your company, and your and your purpose at the beginning of the call.

- Strive to **speak clearly** and at an **understandable rate**

- Try to make a **smile** come through in your voice; have a mirror in front of you so that you can observe your facial expressions.

- Speak in a manner that instills **confidence**.

- Be **courteous**, never argumentative or insulting.

- Maintain a tone of **friendliness**, **enthusiasm**, and **confidence** in your voice regardless of how rough the going may be at times.

- Be **realistic** in your goals.

- Don't make undelivered **promises**.

- If a trial close fails, try to get an **appointment**.

- Take **notes** about what was discussed; it is easy to forget essential points.

(Table 2.5 continued)

- **Evaluate** the likely results of each call; is a follow-up desirable? If so, when?

- Vary your telephone techniques from time to time and **compare results**

Try Videocassettes and Computer Diskettes

A modern method of obtaining new prospects related to mail inquiries is the use of **videocassette and computer diskettes**. One company that manufactures body-building equipment offers in a printed advertisement a 22–minute videocassette that gives the viewer reasons for buying the exercise equipment. A substantial number of leads were developed in that manner. Other companies offer computer diskettes that prospects can view on their personal computers at home or work.

There are some students of prospecting who feel that video cassettes and computer diskettes have their shortcomings, since the viewer must typically watch them from beginning to end. Unfortunately, there may be portions of the tape that are of no interest to the viewer. Regardless of this disadvantage, those who request cassettes or diskettes by mail may furnish salespeople with useful prospecting leads.

Assume that you are a salesperson in the industry of your choice. From what sources might you obtain names of prospective customers?

HOW DO YOU QUALIFY PROSPECTS?

As previously mentioned, virtually everyone is a suspect for your products or services, but a scattershot approach—that is, treating everyone as a prospective customer—can waste a lot of your scarce and valuable time.

A reasonable familiarity with your products, their uses, and their limitations can help in **qualifying prospects**. For example, you would be unlikely to sell many outdoor tropical plants, such as Canary Island Date Palms, to garden stores and nurseries in Great Falls, Montana, or Denver, Colorado. Your products would not be particularly suited to such intemperate climes. Likewise, there is little sense in trying to sell your products to those who have no need or desire for them. It's useful to know for whom and for what your product is designed and to relate your sales presentation to the *needs* of your prospects.

The point is that you should get enough information to enable you to determine if your prospects *qualify* for the purchase of your goods or services. There are five important questions that you should attempt to answer when you are trying to determine good prospects. They are listed in Table 2.6.

Table 2.6 Questions that should be answered when attempting to qualify prospects.

- Does the prospect have a want or need that can be satisfied by the purchase of my products or services?

- Does the prospect have sufficient *purchasing power?*

- Does the prospect have the *authority* to make a purchase?

- Can the prospect be readily *approached*?

- Is the prospect *eligible* to make a purchase?

The act of qualifying prospects separates them from suspects. Qualifying prospects in advance can actually save time later. Let's now turn to a brief examination of each of the above questions.

Does the Prospect Have a Need?

You may have developed a highly convincing sales talk, but you could be wasting valuable time if you're presenting it to someone who has no reason to want or need your product. Some additional questions to ask yourself are these: Is there some way in which the prospect will *benefit* from the purchase of your product? Is there an *actual,* rather than merely a *possible,* need for the product? A prospector for new customers, like a prospector for gold, must sort out the useful from the useless. All that glitters is not gold, warns an old cliche, nor are all suspects potential buyers. Most selling is not done on a one-shot basis. Customers who develop a genuine need for your products and are satisfied with them are likely to be consistent customers. And in many fields, it is the repeat sales that reap long-term benefits.

Can the prospect pay?

Would you appreciate someone trying to pressure you into purchasing an item you couldn't afford? Not likely. Your impression of such an approach would probably be unfavorable. As a salesperson, you should try to avoid overextending prospects by finding out during your preapproach if they can pay for your products.

For example, if you were a real estate salesperson, would there be any point in your attempting to sell a $900,000 to a family whose level of income and wealth would prevent it from qualifying for the necessary loan? However, a caveat is in order: don't assume, without obtaining adequate facts, that a person will not qualify for credit or a purchase. A person's outward appearance can frequently be deceptive. Many sales have been lost because of assumptions based on appearance alone.

Why shouldn't you attempt to qualify a prospect based on his or her appearance?

Is There Authority to Purchase?

Determining who has the specific authority to make buying decisions is sometimes a delicate proposition. Frequently, of course, merely asking your prospect for the names of those involved in the final buying decision can get you the necessary information. But be tactful. And at the same time, don't overlook the *influence* of those who lack actual buying authority. Many people may be involved in the buying process even though they lack official purchasing authority. For example, a supervisor's assistant may exert more influence than the supervisor when it comes to purchasing office equipment.

A serious challenge faced by many salespeople, especially those in selling goods or services to industry, is that many buying decisions today are made by more than one person. Virtually any managers or employees scattered throughout an organization may either directly or indirectly influence purchases.

Sometimes buying decisions are made by established and formal **buying committees**, which, as mentioned in Chapter 1, are ongoing, established groups whose function is to determine the best sources for their organizational purchases.

Can the Prospect be Readily Approached?

"You mean to say that you went to the University of Washington, too?"
"Sure did, College of Bus. Ad., class of '90."
"No kidding. Say did you know Jessica Jackson when you were at the U? Jessica used to date my husband before we were married."

Have you ever heard a conversation something like this? It serves to illustrate another important concept related to prospecting: searching for new customers is far easier when you can approach your prospects under favorable circumstances. Although not always essential for effective results, some prospects are more easily approached if they have backgrounds and interests similar to yours.

Some sales managers feel that young, inexperienced salespeople have more difficulty approaching top management or older prospects. As a result, they often assign more experienced salespeople to key accounts and may even give them impressive titles—such as *account executive, sales manager,* or *marketing vice president*—as a means of adding prestige to their positions. Of course, without the skills to go with them, impressive titles mean little.

Proper timing is also essential in prospecting. If you approach a prospect when she or he is obviously In a bad mood or deeply immersed in a sea of problems, you would be wise to make an appointment for another day. Or if you yourself are in a deeply depressed mood, you might do better to postpone your sales call. The founder of one large companY used to tell his sales representatives that he would rather they sat on a park bench during such periods than create irreparable ill will toward their company.

Is the Prospect Eligible to Buy?

You might answer all of the above questions affirmatively and yet the prospect may still not be able to purchase your product or service. Our last question—Is the prospect eligible to buy?—must also be answered in the affirmative before a sale can take place.

For example, assume that you represent a life insurance company and have contacted Ms. Pam Pamola regarding the purchase of life insurance. Pam, the head of her household, has three dependent children, She wants an ordinary whole life policy, has ample income to pay for it, makes her own buying decisions, and is easy to talk to, but her doctor recently discovered that she has cancer of the esophagus. Because of this, you may not be able to get her the policy she wants, since insurance companies have health standards that must be met before they will issue life insurance policies. Perhaps your prospect would be eligible for a different type of policy.

What are some reasons why some individuals might be ineligible to purchase a particular good or service?

HOW CAN PLANNING AND MAINTAINING ADEQUATE RECORDS ASSIST YOU IN PROSPECTING?

Madre mia! I *thought* there was someone I promised to call on yesterday. How did I ever forget to make that follow-up visit I promised to Mrs. Hotchkiss?

This is a plight that unplanned, disorganized salespeople are likely to find themselves in quite regularly. The need for planning is a concept that cannot be stressed too much. Planning for prospecting activities becomes much easier when you maintain adequate records. Let's now examine some basic ways in which planning and maintaining useful records can help you in your prospecting activities.

Establish a Plan

Successful prospectors generally first establish specific prospecting *objectives* and then develop logical *plans* for accomplishing them. Asking yourself specific questions, such as the following, can also aid in planning:

- Have you decided what prospecting techniques you are going to follow?

- Have you allowed for flexibility in order to match your approach to the personality and needs of the prospect?

- Are you going to send out prospecting letters or use the telephone before making personal calls?

- How much time are you going to set aside for prospecting?

- Have you actually planned specific times for prospecting rather than leave the activity to chance?

Any questions related to effective prospecting should be answered in advance to minimize wasting your scarce time.

Maintain Adequate Records

Effective salespeople usually develop a list of potential customers. A traditional and useful device for keeping track of this list for initial and follow-up calls is a **tickler file**, consisting of 3 x 5 index cards filed by date and serving as a reminder of when you intend to call or follow up on specific prospects and what you are going to discuss. (See Figures 2.4 and 2.5 for sample cards for *householders* and *industrial* purchasers.)

A growing number of salespeople are using computers—either desktop, laptop, notebook, or palmtop models—for prospecting and customer information. Some computers feature such elements as an integrated word processor, telemarketing, autodial, tickler system, call reporting, form letters and mailing labels, and notation space for account profiles. The use of computers can save salespeople substantial amounts of time along with assisting them in the planning and organizing of their preapproach and prospecting activities.

When should a name be deleted from your prospect file?

Name:_____ Spouse's Name:_____

Address:_____ Phone:_____

City:_____ State:_____Zip:_____

Employer:_____ Duties/Title:_____

Spouses Employer:_____ Duties/Title:_____

Children's Names & Ages:_____

Prospect's Personal Interests:_____

Prospect's Potential Needs:_____

_____

Benefits to Be Discussed:_____

Proposed Date of Call:_____

First Call Date:_____

Results, Attitudes, Benefits, Accepted:_____

_____

_____

_____

Follow Up:_____Yes   No_____

If so, when?_____

Follow-up Requirements:_____

_____

References:_____

_____

Figure 2.4 Front (*top*) and back *(bottom)* of a sample prospecting form for householders.

Company Name:_____ Product(s)/Service:_____

Division or Branch:_____

Address:_____ Phone:_____

City:_____ State:_____ Zip:_____

Key Contact Individual:_____ Title:_____

Other Decision Makers:_____ Titles:_____

Purpose of Call:_____

Prospect's Potential Needs:_____

Major Competitors:_____

Have you planned a sales presentation?_____Yes_____No

Benefits to be Discussed:_____

_____

Proposed Date of Call:_____

First Call Date:_____

Results, Attitude, Benefits Accepted:_____

_____

Follow Up?:_____Yes_____No

If so, when?_____

Follow-up Requirements Including Key Decision Makers to Contact:_____

_____

Referrals:_____

_____

Figure 2.5 Front *(top)* and back *(bottom)* of a prospecting form for industrial purchasers.

In many fields, sales are seldom made during the first attempt; callbacks are frequently necessary. Prospects customarily have to be wooed by the salesperson. In effect, there may be what could be considered a courtship period. But don't forget periodically to weed out the names of those who definitely are not prospects.

Rate your prospects

Creative prospectors often rate their prospects. After your initial visit, you may have a fair idea as to how receptive a prospect is to your message. You could rate prospects as hot, medium, or cool or use any other system that indicates to you how much additional effort should be expended on them.

Show appreciation

Prospecting is tough work. It is an activity filled with rebuffs and disappointments. A prospect may not only be cool toward your message but also downright offensive toward you. Sound advice to follow is never to lower yourself to the position of the person who may have insulted or offended you. If you do, you may have reason to regret your actions at a later date.

A practice regularly followed by many successful prospectors is to send thank you letters to every person contacted, an approach that can create substantial goodwill for you and sometimes be a factor in breaking the ice with your prospects.

What is your reaction to the following statement? "I really don't need to prospect. I have all the work I can handle servicing my existing accounts—they've got to come first. So prospecting, for me, would be a waste of my scarce time."

These are terms that you should now be familiar with:

- selling process
- prospecting
- suspects (leads)
- prospects
- preapproach
- endless–chain method
- referral method
- centers of influence
- testimonial letter
- spotters
- sales associates
- cold canvas
- cold calls
- blitz technique
- trade fairs/exhibitions
- clubs
- civic and social groups
- party groups
- surveys
- telemarketing
- telephone and mail inquiries
- video cassettes/computer diskettes
- qualifying prospects
- buying committees
- technique tickler files

CHAPTER 3

APPROACHING PROSPECTIVE CUSTOMERS

When you finish this chapter, you should be able to:

- Create the favorable conditions that are important in approaching buyers.
- Apply the major approach methods for gaining the attention of prospective customers.

CHAPTER 3

We have something in this industry called the 10–3–1 ratio. This means that for every ten calls salespeople make, they will get to make a presentation to three, and if they've got a good success rate, they'll make one sale.

Dennis Tamesin, Senior VP.
Northeastern Mutual Life Insurance

A timid appearing young insurance agent entered the office of a dynamic sales manager, shyly approached the desk, then softly uttered, "You don't want to buy any life insurance, do you?" "No!" snarled the manager. "That's what I was afraid of," sighed the embarrassed agent, starting to leave. "Just wait a minute," demanded the aggressive manager. "I have been dealing with salespeople all my life, and you, without a doubt, are the worst I've ever seen. Don't you realize that you have to inspire confidence, and that to do it you must have confidence in yourself? To help you gain that confidence to make a sale, I'll sign for a $100,000 policy." As he signed the manager advised, "You have to learn some effective techniques for approaching customers and then use them." "Oh, but I have," replied the young agent energetically. "I have an approach for almost every kind of businessperson. The one I just used on you was my standard approach for sales managers!"

This anecdote, although grossly exaggerated (we hope!), helps to illustrate the need for developing creative and imaginative techniques for approaching prospective customers. Startling as it may seem, there are some salespeople whose sales approaches regularly consist of little more than the following: "Good morning, Mr. Green. I'm with the 6L Company and happened to be in the neighborhood. You don't need any supplies today, do you?" Such salespeople may then hear, "My name is Brown, not Green, and you are right—I don't!" So they respond, "Sorry, Mr. Brown. Okay, then, thanks anyway. See you next time I'm in the area. So long."

Salespeople whose styles are consistently no more imaginative than this one generally discover that they need to develop more creative approaches. Those who fail to make this discovery tend to have short–lived careers in the field of selling.

We've already discussed the importance of developing an effective pre approach *(uncovering relevant information about prospects)* and developing a sound prospecting plan *(finding customers)*. Now we arrive at another important step in the selling *process—approaching prospective customers.* The **approach** involves *arranging for interviews and establishing rapport during your initial face–to–face contacts with customers.*

GETTING OFF TO A GOOD START

The approach is the step in the selling process that enables you—the salesperson—to gain the attention of prospective customers so that you will be able to interact with them more favorably and deliver a planned sales presentation. A sound approach, therefore, relates to those activities that help you get off to a good start with customers. And a good start helps to motivate your prospects into wanting to hear your sales message and, especially important, into making affirmative buying decisions.

Yours may be an outstanding product, one designed especially to meet the needs of your customers. But don't be surprised to discover that having a good product doesn't always guarantee that you'll have buyers. You also need to develop a sound approach that will motivate prospects to want to see you. Some prospects tend to have a natural suspicion of strangers—and to a great many prospects, that's exactly what you are: a stranger.

Maintaing Customer Satisfaction

Closing the Sale

Overcoming Sales Resistance

Presenting and Demonstrating the Sales Message

Approaching Prospective Customers 3

Finding Qualified Customers (Prospecting)

Figure 3.1 Approaching prospective customers is the second activity in the selling process.

Getting off to a good start with an imaginative approach can be tremendously helpful to you in the selling process. Your sales record is likely to reflect the skillfulness of your efforts in this area. The following section presents some of the more significant factors that should be considered when approaching prospective customers.

Appointments—To Make or Not to Make

Should you always make appointments before a sales call, or can you ever simply drop by to see a customer unannounced? Generally, normal courtesy dictates that appointments be made, either by telephone, letter, or prior personal contact. However, in some types of selling, such as house–to–house selling, making appointments in advance is often impractical. Furthermore, prospects unfamiliar with you or your products are sometimes hesitant to agree to a specific appointment. And prospects contacted for the first time find it relatively easy to refuse attempts at making appointments over the telephone.

Some customers rarely object to your dropping by without an appointment, especially if you have something useful to offer. However, you should not make a call unless you do have something to say or show that can truly benefit your customer. Most customers do not appreciate your dropping by merely to "rap about nothing."
One of the major advantages of having an advance appointment is that you are likely to *gain more complete attention* from your customers, since they generally will be mental set to see you and thus more receptive to your message. Contacting customers without an appointment, when they are preoccupied with other activities, leaves your sales message competing for their attention.

When asking a prospect or customer for an appointment, always make it as easy as possible for him or her to make a decision. Inexperienced salespeople might ask something like, "Ms. Swartzplat, when might be a good time for me to call on you." Ms. Swartzplat, in this instance, has nothing specific to grab onto, and it becomes easier for her to respond negatively to the request.

72

A more effective approach would be, "Ms. Swartzplat, I'm going to be working in your area next Tuesday. I have some information that will be of interest to you. I could see you at 9:30 A.M., or would 1:30 P.M. be better?" You have made it easy for Ms. Swartzplat to make a decision, and if she indicates that she is busy at both times, you could ask, "When would be a more convenient time for you?"

What's wrong with the following approach to securing an appointment? "Mr. Harcourt, I'm going to be working in your area next week. When might be a good time to drop in to tell you about our new line of products?"

Some sales representatives find it helpful to send a letter or postcard to the prospective customer as a reminder of the upcoming appointment.

Butterflies in the Tummy

Your moods and attitudes, which are a part of your overall appearance, are extremely important when you make your first calls on prospective customers. Salespeople, especially before making their first calls in the morning, sometimes feel as though they were marching off to a perilous battlefield.

Take the example of Bonnie Dewar: Bonnie, a representative of a large garment manufacturing firm, is about to make her first sales call of the day on the buyer of a medium–sized department store. It is Monday morning. Her weekend was enjoyably spent with her family, and she was in high spirits when she left home this morning. Bonnie has driven to within three blocks of her customer's store, and suddenly she feels some frightening changes in her emotional state coming over her. The rate of her heartbeat has quickened, and her mouth feels as though her salivary glands had gone on a wildcat strike. Bonnie's mouth is so dry that she feels as though its roof and floor were about to fuse. Her sweat glands, working overtime, seem to be making up for the loss of activity in her salivary glands. Her forehead, palms, and underarms are moist with perspiration Bonnie wonders if maybe she shouldn't have kept her job flipping hamburgers in a fast–food restaurant!

Although a bit exaggerated, Bonnie's emotional reactions are typical of what salespeople occasionally feel to one degree or another. You might find it consoling to realize that a certain amount of tension and nervousness, especially before your first call of the day, is not only natural but even somewhat beneficial. Such emotional feelings are likely to be evidence that your have a sincere concern for your performance. And concerned sales representatives are generally far better prepared for their sales presentations than those who are indifferent toward their activities.

Excessive, uncontrollable nervousness, however, could be the result of insufficient experience in selling or inadequate preparation for a specific sales call. With *greater experience and more effective planning, you* should find that your tensions lessen and your confidence increases. But don't be particularly concerned about occasional feelings of anxiety—It's unlikely that they'll be eliminated completely. Experienced sales people realize that they "go with the territory" and learn to accept and live with such feelings.

What advice might be offered to a young salesperson who has expressed feelings of nervousness before making first sales each day?

Your Shoes Are Showing

A salesperson's appearance communicates various messages to prospective customers. There are enough hurdles for you to overcome when approaching prospects without beginning with the handicap of an appearance that is unacceptable to your customers. Rational or not, many people do tend to form first impressions of a salesperson based on his or her wearing apparel and grooming. As the Queen of England once wrote to her son, the Prince of Wales:

Dress gives one the outward sign from which people in general can, and often do, judge upon the inward state of mind and feelings of a person; for this they *can see;* while the other they *cannot see.* On that account, clothes are of particular importance...[1]

Recognize, too, that standards of dress vary with the industry and territory. There are no hard and fast rules for dress that can apply to every situation. What might be an acceptable standard of dress in downtown San Francisco could seem bizarre in the desert town of El Centro. Some organizations prefer to convey a conservative image to their customers; others prefer a more modern one.

Why is a your appearance—wearing apparel and grooming—so important to your sales accomplishments?

Wearing apparel and grooming, however, are only part of the total *impression* that salespeople make on prospective customers. Something as seemingly insignificant as a business card can affect your image before a prospect. For example, you're probably off to a bad start if you hand the prospect a crumpled or grimy card instead of a neat, fresh–appearing one.

Your sales aids also contribute toward the total impression you are making. You've probably lost some ground with your prospect if your sales aids are shop–worn and tattered looking. Even your appointment book makes an impression. Is it bulging with disorganized looking scraps of paper, or is it neat and not distracting to the prospect?

And finally, how about the seats and floor of your car? Are they littered with messy odds and ends? When you take your prospect somewhere in your car, do you generally have to apologize for the mess while you attempt to hurriedly straighten it up before you can drive on?

Remember that *everything* you wear, carry, and do influences the prospect's perception of you and your company. Appearances that may seem insignificant do have an effect on the total impression you make on your prospective customers.

I'm Sorry I'm Late

Concerned salespeople, especially those who are well organized, seldom arrive late for appointments. Those who do arrive late often get off to a bad start with their customers. Prospective buyers, expecting you to arrive at specific times, will sometimes postpone other projects in anticipation of your visit. Any time spent waiting for you is wasted time for them—they could have been doing other things. To avoid this problem, plan to arrive at least ten minutes before an appointment; this allows time for possible delays, such as those caused by traffic congestion. Struggling through highway traffic when you are late for an appointment can create additional tensions and frustrations that can do little but detract from your sales delivery.

Do you agree or disagree that arriving on time is not as important as having a good product and a well-organized sales presentation? Why?

Dealing with Multiple Decision Makers

In some types of selling situations, especially in industrial selling, **multiple buying decisions** are quite common. Many buying decisions today are made by more than one person. As mentioned in Chapter 1, sometimes they're made by established and formal **buying committees**.

A related concept is the **buying center**, which represents all the people who either directly or indirectly influence purchases. The buying center is not considered a formal group or place. Instead, it could consist of virtually any managers or employees scattered throughout the organization.

What is the difference between a buying committee and a buying center?

In some instances, as many as 5 to 20 people may be a part of the buying center and have to be "sold" before a final buying decision is made. Most of them are not typically a part of the purchasing department of the industrial customer. Instead, they might be production line personnel who are final users of the product, or they could be specific managers or employees who have been formally assigned final purchasing authority. They could even be secretaries and receptionists who are in the strategic position of being able to influence the flow of information to industrial purchasers with final buying authority. For example, a boss' assistant could be more significant than the boss in determining which brand of computer or software will be purchased. Such a person might also provide you with useful information that could assist you in making a sale to the actual decision makers.

The way you can approach such prospective buyers is discussed in the following section on intermediaries.

Behavior with Intermediaries

As implied above, when making a sale call you ordinarily will not see the prospective purchaser immediately. More typical is an initial greeting from an intermediary, such as an assistant, secretary, or receptionist. Intermediaries are sometimes referred to as **gatekeepers**. These are individuals who determine what information is received by key decision makers. Curtness or lack of tact and consideration toward such individuals can frequently result in lost sales. Intermediaries are frequently a part of the buying center, and thus can have far more influence with their bosses than you might realize. Study the ground rules in Table 3.1. They should be considered when dealing with intermediaries in order to avoid harming your chances of securing a favorable interview with the actual buyer.

Table 3.1 Guidelines for approaching intermediaries.

- Try to make a favorable impression on the intermediary. Introduce yourself and your company, possibly presenting the intermediary with your business card and some of your company literature.

- Have a positive, courteous attitude, and don't forget to present a genuine smile.

- Don't waste the intermediary's time with idle chatter or flirtation. He or she also has job responsibilities.

- Don't waste your own time. Waiting can give you an opportunity to catch up on certain activities, such as planning, studying company literature (either yours or your prospect's), or preparing sales reports.

- Be businesslike while waiting. Idly daydreaming or restlessly tapping your hand on your notebook computer is likely to create anything but a favorable impression.

Bypassing the Receptionist

Office protocol generally assumes that outsiders who call on organizations will first check with the receptionist. Some salespeople feel that dealing with receptionists can waste time, especially when the customer is well known and friendly. But any salesperson who bypasses formal channels should be certain to know his or her customers well and avoid the practice in situations where it might be considered rude.

Should you ever bypass a receptionist and go directly to your prospects office or desk?

How Long to Wait

Occasionally you may have an appointment for a specific time, but your customer makes you wait. Above all, try not to display impatience or anger while waiting. However, the question sometimes arises as to how long you should wait. Your time is also valuable, and time spent waiting is time not spent selling.

Many sales managers advise their sales team to use sound judgment. Under most circumstances you should not wait much longer than 10 to 15 minutes. If your prospect hasn't seen you within 15 minutes, there is a possibility that he or she has forgotten about you. Rather than continue waiting and wasting your selling time, you could inform the receptionist that you have another appointment and ask how soon your customer will be available. If the customer will be occupied for some time, you could request another appointment.

Sometimes, of course, waiting is necessary, especially when an important buyer is unavoidably detained. As with any situation in selling, you should use your judgment in determining how long to wait for a specific customer. In any case, since you are destined to spend portions of your working day waiting, you could make effective use of this time by planning future activities or studying.

Create a Receptive Atmosphere

Let's assume that you are a manufacturer's representative for a printing products company. You have called upon Black and Blue Ink, Inc., a dealership in your territory that purchases a variety of items for resale in the printing trades. The person responsible for prospective purchases is Henry Senefelder, an affable individual who was recently promoted to his present position with Black and Blue.

Those first few moments with your prospective customer, Mr. Senefelder, are extremely important, since they will set the tone for the entire sales interview. Remember that he's probably been thinking of everything but your mission. So if your presentation is going to be received and understood by Senefelder, you are going to have to get him into a frame of mind that wants to listen to your message.

Table 3.2 Topics to avoid when attempt to develop rapport with your customers.

- Avoid talking merely for the sake of talking.

- Avoid telling ethnic or gay–bashing type jokes.

- Avoid discussing partisan political issues.

- Avoid discussing emotion–packed issues, such as gun control and legalized abortion.

- Avoid talking only about your own interests

A certain amount of *rapport–building conversation* related to the buyer's interests and hobbies can sometimes serve to break the ice, but you should be careful not to appear phony or to be talking merely for the sake of talking. Your immediate goal should be to create rapport with Senefelder. This part of the interview becomes quite natural when you have a sincere interest in your customers.

A few "should nots": you should not attempt to establish rapport by telling ethnic or gay–bashing type jokes. Even if your prospect positively is not a member of such groups, he or she may have strong concerns in this area and feel that you are somewhat offensive. To be on the safe side, some managers advise that their salespeople avoid telling any jokes. If your joke fails to go over with the prospect, you place him or her in the awkward position of having to feign a laugh in order to humor or be polite to you. Nor should you assume that all of your prospective customers are interested in sports just because you are. Politics is another subject that can result in unwanted differences, with possibly animosity and lost sales, between prospects and you. Emotional issues, too, such as legalized abortion or gun control, are better off not discussed during your time with prospective customers. A better approach is to ask probing questions that can aid you in uncovering your prospect's true interests. Most people enjoy talking about their own interests and activities. You may bore them, however, if you talk only about your own interests. And you may anger them with your expressed political or personal points of view.

What sort of conversations are you better off avoiding when attempting to develop rapport with your customer?

The Need for Self–Assurance

You certainly don't want to appear cocky or arrogant when with prospects, nor do you need to appear apologetic for taking a portion of their time.

Some sales representatives unthinkingly open with such comments as, "I'm sorry to bother you, Mr. Hernandez." One prospective buyer confronted with this approach wryly retorted, "Well, I'd hate to see you do something you are sorry for, so I'll see you some other time!"

80

Remember why you call on potential customers. You have products or services that can benefit them. You are there to serve and assist your customers with their problems and needs. If you sincerely see your responsibility as one of serving your customers, you are likely to discover that they see you the same way.

Foreign sales representatives, unfamiliar with American culture, have sometimes aroused undue suspicion in American buyers. For example, extreme politeness and humility are features of some cultures. And bowing, accompanied by humility, is considered normal within some groups. But Americans, typically unaccustomed to such behavior, sometimes feel uncomfortable in excessively formal situations.

You should attempt to tailor your approach and role to meet the style and expectations of the prospect. Acceptable behavior includes appearing reasonably confident, poised, and courteous.

A wise, but anonymous, philosopher once said, "Manners are the oil that lubricates civilized existence." Try to paraphrase the statement in your own words.

HOW CAN YOU GAIN THE ATTENTION OF YOUR CUSTOMERS?

Let's assume that all has gone well so far. The receptionist has informed you that your customer will see you in a few moments. The curtain is about to rise and your debut to commence. Your opportunity to perform the skills of your trade has arrived at last. Now begins a crucial part of the approach phase of the selling process—gaining *the attention* of your prospective buyer.

How you perform now will significantly influence the success or failure of your presentation. The attention you seek must, of course, be favorable and should make the prospect more receptive to your presentation. It certainly should not be merely attention for attention's sake.

One of your principal objectives at this stage of the selling process is motivating and guiding your prospect into making a favorable buying decision. Your prospect is unlikely to make a favorable buying decision, however, until enough information is received to justify one. And the information can't be received unless he or she pays attention to your presentation.

Sometimes getting the attention of the buyer is no trouble at all. In fact, you may be cordially greeted with something like, "Hello, you're just the person I was thinking about. I have an order here I'd like you to quote me some prices on." At other times, there may be numerous distractions competing for the buyer's attention. Here is where empathy on your part becomes significant. If you were in the prospect's shoes, what would attract your interest and attention? How have successful salespeople overcome this hurdle? Some of the proven methods used to capture the buyer's interest are discussed below. (See Table 3.3 for a summary of methods.)

Table 3.3 Approach methods used to capture the interest of potential buyers.

- Compliment the customer
- Appeal to curiosity
- Question the buyer
- Provide a free service
- Present useful ideas
- Present customer benefits
- Solve customer problems

- Use OK names.
- Offer samples and gifts
- Use the product approach
- Use referrals
- Use element of surprise
- Use showmanship

Compliment the Customer

Most people enjoy recognition and the feeling of self–esteem, so **complimenting customers** can be an effective way to capture a buyer's interest. If you have done your homework properly, you might know of significant achievements or events related to your prospects or their firms. For example, you may have learned that your customer, Casper Sodaberger and his wife recently gave birth to a baby girl. You might say something like, "Casper, I hear you recently became the proud father of a baby girl. Congratulations! What did you name her?" Or perhaps the buyer's firm has developed a new product, received public recognition for a recent activity, or has an unusually attractive store layout. Merely remembering and using the customer's name could be considered a way of complimenting the customer.

A sincere compliment can often enhance your initial approach. But the compliment itself is not enough; it must be *sincere, believable,* and *specific.* You should avoid any compliments that will sound insincere to the prospect.

In what way should you be careful when employing the complimenting–customers approach?

Appeal to Curiosity

Another approach used to gain attention relates to the human tendency to be curious. An action or an opening statement with **curiosity appeal** can pave the way to a more effective demonstration.

For example, a question that would probably arouse interest is: "Mr. Marner, if I could show you a system for reducing by twenty percent the cost of each letter mailed from your office, would you be interested" Of course your prospect would be interested in saving money, and Mr. Marner would probably be willing to give you some time if your approach seemed sincere and honest.

Occasionally you may plan to use a visual aid, such as a portable videocassette player, in your sales presentation. If you do so, you can often arouse curiosity by not immediately saying what the visual aid is. Some salespeople, for example, arouse curiosity by placing the object, still in its container, on the floor beside the desk. The prospect often asks, "What's in the box?" The salesperson can then respond with a smile and say, "Filbert, I'm glad you asked. Inside this container is an idea that can eliminate one of your most severe production problems."

Question the Buyer

Do you remember when your professor at college asked questions in class? Even if you weren't being called on, or the questions were merely rhetorical, didn't the quizzical sound of a question tend to draw you into the discussion? Effective speakers frequently use the **questioning approach** to create or maintain interest even when an answer isn't expected. In opening sales calls, probing questions are often used. For example, assume that you sent a letter to a prospect in advance of your visit. As an attention–getter, you might ask something like, "Ms. Clipson, what was your reaction to the plan discussed in the recent letter I sent to you?" Even if Ms. Clipson doesn't remember the letter, your initial question has paved the way for additional questions.

Provide a Free Service

One of the most effective ways of opening a sales call is to offer a **free service**. This approach can serve as tangible evidence of your sincere interest in the customer and usually arouses his or her attention. One company's sales trainees are advised to use the service approach is this fashion: "My reason for calling on you today, Mr. Lopez, is to check on the inventory control system we set up for ordering replacement products from our firm." Salespeople calling on retailers often use this approach—they offer to check inventory needs or to set up promotional displays as a service to the buyers. Some representatives even offer to demonstrate their products—cameras or wall covering materials, for example—to the customers of retail outlets.

Present Useful

Ideas Your customers are continually looking for new ideas. Ultimate consumers want to know how they can operate their households more efficiently. Businesses are interested in methods for reducing costs and increasing profits.

If you were a manager, of, say, a retail store, wouldn't you be likely to be receptive to ideas that could help you in your operations? Most managers would be. During regular sales calls, salespeople are likely to learn of merchandising techniques and uses for their products that have proven effective for their customers. As a method of gaining attention, some of these **useful ideas** could be passed on to other customers during the approach. A favorable opening remark designed to develop the interest of your customers could be, "Mr. Hooper, the other day I came across an idea that resulted in a 10 percent increase in cash flow for a firm similar to yours. Here's how it works."

How might you apply the useful idea approach with prospective customers?

Present Customer Benefits

Related to presenting useful ideas is the **customer–benefit approach**. When using this technique, you would make a statement or raise a question that enables the prospect to realize how he or she can benefit from the purchase of your product or service.

For example, assume that you sell document transmission systems known in the industry as facsimile, or fax, machines. Yours is called the FAX–325i. It enables businesses to send and receive documents, graphics, and halftone photos anywhere in the world over telephone lines.

You might say something like this to your customer: "Mr. Replique, here's a significant benefit that the FAX–325i business facsimile unit provides: At the touch of one button, the FAX–325i can speed–dial up to forty–nine locations. Coded speed–dialing allows access to one hundred more. Its high–speed transmission capability sends crisp, clear, picture–perfect

85

documents to their destinations almost instantly—ten seconds per page—at the mere cost of a phone call. With this unit, your document transmission costs are cut to a minimum." (Of course, you would want to be certain that your prospect understood the terminology associated with document transmitting systems before using such jargon.)

Solve Customer Problems

Similar to the customer–benefit and questioning approaches is the **problem-solving approach**. Most prospects have problems. And it should be safe to state that most prospects would like to rid themselves of these problems. Prospects, especially commercial buyers, often don't perceive their actions as buying a particular brand of merchandise or service. Instead, their purchases are perceived more as an activity intended to create solutions to specific problems.

How do your customers' problems relate to their willingness to be receptive to your sales message?

Of course, you must discover what your prospects' problems are, which can be done through the skillful use of questioning and listening techniques. One effective method of getting prospects' attention during the approach, therefore, is to ask them to tell you what their biggest problem is. This approach will usually motivate most prospects, who generally are glad to talk about the problems with which they're currently wrestling. It also helps them to release some of their stress by "getting it off their chests." Later in your presentation you can demonstrate how your product or service will solve their real problems.

Use "OK Names"

Some prospects are favorably impressed when they learn that well–known companies are using your products." The use of **"OK names"**—that is, names of firms that are known and respected by your prospects—can often favorably influence your own customers. (Typically you should obtain permission from existing customers before revealing their personal activities to prospective customers.)

86

Using *testimonial letters* (as discussed in the previous chapter) is related to this approach and can help you secure your buyer's interest and attention.

Offer Samples and Gifts

In some types of selling, offering product **samples** or **gifts** is quite commonplace. For example, some salespeople open by saying, "Ms. Fisk, I have an appointment organizer for you that I hope you will find useful." Salespersons with pharmaceutical companies generally pass out product samples and literature to doctors and pharmacists. Perfume company representatives often offer free miniature bottles of perfume to prospective buyers. Samples and gifts not only arouse interest and attention but are also useful as selling tools that appeal to a buyer's senses.

Product Approach

Another method for arousing interest is the **product approach**. With this technique you simply hand your product or demonstration model to the prospective customer and wait for a reaction. In a sense, you're allowing the product to gain the prospect's attention and arouse his or her interest. After handling the prospect the product, say nothing—merely listen. The reaction that you get from the prospect will be a clue as to what your next actions should be. Questions from the prospect regarding price or product availability, for example, could be an indication of a sincere interest in making a purchase. The product approach is best used with products that have certain unique or appealing features likely to attract the prospect's attention.

How might the product approach aid you in approaching customers?

If the product itself isn't available, brochures, merchandising pieces, cutaway models, or even a special part of the product can be used to capture the prospect's attention and interest. Be certain before your interview that your model is in good working order.

Use Referrals

"Mr. Chung," last week I was talking with a friend of yours, Jim Murphy, and he told me that you might be interested in an idea that we put work for him with astonishing success." This is an example of the **referral approach**, a technique that can be extremely useful for gaining the interest of your prospective customer, especially when he or she has great respect for the person giving the referral. Some salespeople also use **blind referrals**—for example, "Ms. Felps, a number of our customers have told us...."

How might you use the referral approach when contacting prospective customers?

Use Element of Surprise

Imagine the reaction of a prospect if you sold computer work stations and opened with the comment, "You, Mr. Harper, like everyone else, are concerned these days with rising costs." It seems as though the price of everything has soared sky high, and we're all looking for ways to cut costs. I would like to demonstrate a computer work station system to you that is four times *more expensive* than any system you've purchased previously." Mr. Harper might first wonder if he had heard you correctly. The **surprise** approach could be an effective attention getter. He might ask, "Did you say four times *more* expensive?" You could then explain that although the system is more expensive initially, its features would actually result in cost reductions because of more efficient operations, storage and retrieval capabilities, lower maintenance costs, greater flexibility, and a higher trade–in value.

Use Showmanship

Although the term *showmanship is* often associated with the entertainment field, the professional salesperson can also apply the concept to his or her own benefit. Showmanship is considered as having a flair for dramatic or visual effectiveness; it does not mean behaving like a clown before the prospect.

88

To illustrate, a person selling an expensive line of porcelain dinnerware has successfully used what could be called a **showmanship approach** with customers. This salesperson places a delicate–appearing dish on the floor and asks prospects to stand on it to demonstrate its durability. As yet, not one dish has broken, and the prospects are generally fascinated by such an unusual approach. If the unexpected did occur, however, and a dish did break, the salesperson could be ready with a humorous comment, such as, "I knew I shouldn't have eaten that extra pancake this morning!"

These approaches are only some of the many that can be used to attract the attention of your prospects and customers. You should experiment with new techniques from time to time and vary your approach in order to avoid repetition with the same customers.

These are terms and concepts that you should now be familiar with:

- approach

- multiple buying decisions

- buying committees

- buying center

- gatekeepers

- complimenting–customers approach

- referral approach

- blind referral

- surprise approach

- showmanship approach

- useful–idea approach

- customer–benefit approach

- problem–solving approach

- "OK–names" approach

- sample/gift approach

- product approach

- curiosity–appeal approach

- questioning approach

- free–service approach

NOTE

1. Mortimer Levitt, *The Executive Look and How to Get It* (New York: AMACOM, n.d.), p. 10.

CHAPTER 4

PRESENTING YOUR SALES MESSAGE

When you finish this chapter, you should be able to:

• Explain the purpose of planning and developing an effective sales presentation.

• Utilize the major characteristics of a well–planned presentation.

• Resolve the major types of problems that tend to arise during sales presentations.

• Develop an effective sales presentation of your own.

CHAPTER 4

A benefit isn't a benefit unless it meets a specific need.

Dennis Hawver
President, RHR Institute

Let's assume that you've done a formidable job of prospecting, have uncovered necessary and relevant information about your potential buyer during your preapproach, and have developed an approach so powerful and persuasive that it would melt the heart of Ebenezer Scrooge, even convincing him to shout "Merry Christmas!" from the rooftops. Your appearance, of course, is impeccable—shoes shined, clothes pressed—and your prospect appears receptive and relaxed after a reasonable amount of informal conversation. You seem to have aroused a desired amount of curiosity for your product. In short, everything seems to be going precisely as you had hoped.

Suddenly, however, you're filled with fright. You're looking at the prospect, Ms. Anthrop, and she's looking expectantly at you. Ms. Anthrop suddenly exclaims, "Don't just sit there—say something!" You then realize that you forgot one "small" detail; you neglected learning about the next important step in the sales process: *how to make an effective sales presentation.*

All is not lost, however. Through the mystical powers of imagination we can extricate you from your plight and start you on a journey designed to get you to your sales destination. After your imaginary but harrowing experience with Ms. Anthrop, you should realize the importance of preparing a well–planned **sales presentation**, one that appeals to the needs of your prospects and that helps you with that crucial step in the selling process: the close.

Maintaing Customer Satisfaction

Closing the Sale

Overcoming Sales Resistance

Presenting and Demonstrating the Sales Message 4

Approaching Prospective Customers

Finding Qualified Customers (Prospecting)

Figure 4.1 Presenting the sales message is another activity in the selling process.

In this chapter we examine and evaluate some of the principal types of sales presentations, provide specific suggestions for improving them, and discuss a number of the more common obstacles or problems you may face when delivering your sales message. The next chapter discusses a related topic: demonstrating with sales aids to create more dramatic sales presentations.

WHY PLANNED SALES PRESENTATIONS ARE IMPORTANT

Ask some sales representatives what type of sales presentations they use and you might be given a quizzical stare followed by, "What type? Heck, I don't have any fancy ivory–tower name for my sales presentations. I'll leave the labels to those college profs who don't have anything better to do. I just see my customers and sell, that's all!"

There may be some salespeople who have no planned presentations and merely "play it by ear." But in today's modern, complex, and competitive world, most well–managed organizations have highly organized sales training programs; in these, sales trainees study and practice some of the proven types of sales presentations in order to develop selling skills. Most sales managers today feel that without planned presentations, salespeople are likely to waste considerable amounts of their own and their prospective customers' time.

How might you employ both a planned sales presentation and situational selling simultaneously?

"Find a need and fill it," was for along time a slogan affixed to the sides of cement trucks of a large sand and gravel company. These words more or less summarize the major purpose of any sales presentation. As the slogan implies, the primary purpose of any presentation should be:

- To arouse in the prospective customer a feeling of need, desire, or availability of a solution to a problem.

- To show how your product can fill or satisfy the customer's recognized need or desire, or provide solutions to his or her problems.

95

Stated another way, the major purpose of the sales presentation is to get prospective customers to realize how they *need* and can *benefit* from what you have to offer, or how you can provide *solutions* to their *problems*.

What is the major purpose of a sales presentation? On what should it mainly focus?

In reality, a sales presentation begins with the *approach,* the step in the selling process designed initially to get the prospect to want to see you and to arouse his or her interest and attention so that you can deliver your sales message. A planned presentation can help you *maintain* the buyer's interest. It should also help you *uncover customer needs and problems.* Both can facilitate your major objective—creating a *desire* for your product or service. Buyer objections, which occur regularly during presentations, and techniques for closing sales, are covered in separate chapters. Now let's move on to a description of the characteristics and types of sales presentations typically used by sales representatives today.

CHARACTERISTICS OF EFFECTIVE PRESENTATIONS

A planned presentation should not imply inflexibility. In fact, experienced salespeople usually employ what can be termed situational selling, the process of drawing on past sales experiences and knowledge when confronting a prospective buyer while recognizing at the same time that each selling situation is unique. It is an activity, therefore, that requires flexibility and imagination.

Without prior planning and rehearsal, you will be less likely to make an effective presentation or to develop high–level selling skills. You should know in advance what you want to accomplish and how you intend to go about it. (See Table 4.1 for a checklist for planning sales calls on commercial or industrial prospects.) Before you can develop an effective sales presentation, however, you must be familiar with the essential elements of the typical sales message.

Table 4.1 Checklist for planning sales calls on commercial or industrial prospects.

1. Company name and address of prospect:

   _____

2. Relevant information already known about the organization's operations:

   _____

3. Relevant information known about organization's buying policies and procedures:

   _____

4. Key personnel (and titles) to call on:

   _____

5. Purpose of sales call:

   _____

6. Previous calls (dates and result)

   _____

7. Competitors already positioned with this firm:

   _____

8. Advantages and disadvantages enjoyed by the competition:

   _____

9. Needs, wants, and problems existing in this firm that could be satisfied or solved by your products or service:

   _____

10. Opening technique planned to arouse customer interest:

    _____

11. Key points you intend to make in your presentation:

    _____

(Table 4.1 continued)

12. Proof for backing up your claims:

_____

13. Principal types of objections anticipated:

_____

14. Method for asking for order

_____

The AIDCA Concept

A classic sales concept that most selling professionals are familiar with is the **AIDCA concept** (originally referred to as *AIM).* According to proponents of AIDCA, the salesperson should attempt to guide the prospect's mind through *five stages,* or steps, leading to a buying decision. The goal of each of these stages is to secure the customer's *attention;* arouse the customer's *interest;* stimulate the customer's *desire* for your product or service; help the customer develop *conviction,* or belief, in your product or service; and obtain *action* or a *buying decision* from the buyer. These steps are summarized in Figure 4.2.

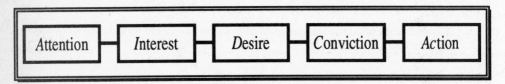

Figure 4.2 The five mental stages, or steps, through which a salesperson attempts to guide a prospective customer.

These stages are referred to as the AIDCA concept, an acronym made up from the first letter of each stage. Although the customer is not consciously aware of the five steps, the salesperson, in effect, guides the prospect through each one in order to make a sale.

Secure *Attention*

The *first step* involves securing your prospect's *attention,* which should take place as early as possible during the interview. You can't get very far in selling a prospect something unless you have his or her attention. Undivided attention isn't always easy to acquire. Securing the necessary attention is going to be especially difficult if your prospect's mind is preoccupied with something else or burdened with problems or pressures. If you sense that you can't readily obtain a prospect's attention at a particular time, maybe you'd better make an appointment for another time when he or she will be more receptive to your message.

Arouse *Interest*

After you get your prospect's attention, the *second step* in AIDCA is to try to arouse his or her *interest* in the meaning of your message. The previous chapter on the approach discussed various ways to gain both the interest and attention of prospects. You might gain interest through a sound choice of words or perhaps through graphic means, such as charts or other types of visual aids (to be discussed more fully in the following chapter). As we'll see shortly, focusing on *customer needs* and *problems* along with product *benefits* is apt to arouse the prospect's interest in your message.

Stimulate *Desire*

The *third step* in AIDCA is attempting to stimulate your prospective customer into having a *desire* to do something related to your proposal. Without a desire—that is, the feeling of wanting your product or service— the next two steps are unlikely to follow.

Develop *Conviction*

Sometimes your prospects may have an interest in your product or service, but deep down inside, they're just not yet convinced that they should take the big step and make a buying decision. In other words, they don't yet have complete *conviction,* or a strong enough *belief,* that they need your product or service or that it is the one that will satisfy their needs or desires. Your efforts, therefore, must be in the direction of aiding the potential buyer in eliminating any doubts that your product or service is the one that should be purchased. Your prospects are likely to be ready to buy once they have entered the mental stage of conviction.

*A*ction—A Buying Decision

After you have successfully guided the prospective purchaser through the previous four steps, you must then ask him or her to buy—that is engage in action. Doing so is not so difficult as sometimes imagined. Later chapters will provide you with specific suggestions on how to guide the buyer through the various mental steps, or stages, that prospects go through before making a final buying decision.

Summarize in your own words the purpose and general nature of the AIDCA concept.

Put Some FUN–FAB OPTIC into Your Sales Life

In training salespeople, one of the things professional sales managers and trainers usually try to encourage their trainees to avoid is focusing on a product's features during a sales presentation. As we'll see shortly, most salespeople are advised instead to incorporate into their sales presentations elements that we'll refer to as the **FUN–FAB OPTIC** concept.

101

F i r s t
　　U n c o v e r
　　N e e d s

F e a t u r e s
　　A d v a n t a g e s
　　B e n e f i t s

O b j e c t i o n s
　P r o v i n g
　　T r i a l C l o s i n g
　　I n s u r i n g
　　　C l o s i n g

Figure 4.3 The FUN–FAB OPTIC concept, which represents the essential elements of a sales presentation.

As you can see in Figure 4.3, the FUN part of FUN–FAB stands for *First Uncover Needs*. The FAB stands for *Features, Advantages*, and *Benefits*. The OPTIC represents *Objections, Proving, Trial* closing, *Insuring*, and *Closing*. The acronym FUN–FAB OPTIC gives you a mental handle that can help you to recall the essential features of a sales presentation. Let's now see if we can shed some light on all this alphabet soup.

Let's Have Some FUN

One of the most common mistakes made by inexperienced salespeople is stressing the *features* and *advantages* of their products before they understand the prospective customer's *needs*. Let's pretend for the moment that we are observing a personable young sales representative—Mark Tyme is his name—who works for a computer supply and equipment firm. Mark means well, but unfortunately he hasn't yet received adequate sales training. As we observe Mark, we see that he has already established reasonable rapport with his prospect, Ms. Dee Kline. Mark leads into his sales presentation by saying: Ms Kline, I want to point out to you what I believe is one of the outstanding *features* of this Microgood Silent–Tone Laser Sx1 PreScript printer—its natural gray color. Our product developers feel that gray really enhances the appearance of the printer. I also want to emphasize one of the specific *advantages* that this printer has over many other printers, namely, the ability to utilize 13 scalable typefaces.

What did Mark overlook when he stressed how sold *he* was on the gray color and the advantages of 13 scalable typefaces? He failed to ask questions to uncover information related to the needs, desires, and attitudes of the customer.

Will Mark's customer, Ms. Dee Kline, necessarily feel that the gray color is an outstanding feature solely because Mark feels that way? Does Ms. Kline have a recognized need for a printer that can employ 13 scalable typefaces? It's difficult for Mark to know for certain unless he probes. The important point to be remembered in the FUN part of FUN–FAB OPTIC is that before you stress something that may be irrelevant or unimportant to a prospect, you should carefully *ask questions* to uncover his or her *needs* and *wants*. Now try to reinforce your understanding of the FUN segment by carefully examining Figure 4.4.

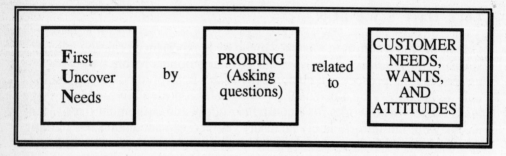

| First Uncover Needs | by | PROBING (Asking questions) | related to | CUSTOMER NEEDS, WANTS, AND ATTITUDES |

Figure 4.4 The elements of the FUN segment of the FUN–FAB OPTIC concept.

Here are two examples of questions intended to uncover need or wants:

- Mr. Training Director, what do you generally look for in a quality laser printer?"

- "What are the major limitations of the printer that you're currently using in your office?"

Make It FAB

Now comes the second part—FAB—of our acronym FUN–FAB–OPTIC. Remember that FAB stands for *F*eatures, *A*dvantages, and *B*enefits. One of your main goals after you've uncovered the prospect's needs and attitudes is to convert your products' **features** and **advantages** into **benefits** that relate to the customer's **needs**.

For example, let's assume that you are an automobile salesperson. During the FUN phase of your sales presentation, you've learned that the prospect is on an extremely tight budget—and you have a car that should satisfy this need for economy. It *features* a 1.6 liter engine. One of its *advantages* is that it can be driven farther than many other cars on a given amount of gasoline. How, therefore, might you convert those factors into customer benefits? Basically, they add up to the *benefit* of reduced operating costs.

Which of the three factors is probably the most important to the customer—the engine *feature,* the *advantage* of greater mileage per gallon of gasoline, or the *benefit* of reduced operating costs. The latter, the reduced–cost benefit, would tend to be a major factor influencing the customer's buying decisions. See Figure 4.5 for an illustration of this concept.

Features **A**dvantages **B**enefits	compose the process of	COVERTING FEATURES AND ADVANTAGES INTO CUSTOMER BENEFITS

Figure 4.5 The Elements of the FAB segment of the FUN–FAB OPTIC concept.

Convince with OPTIC

Now we're concerned with the last part of the FUN–FAB OPTIC memory jogger. As a reminder, OPTIC stands for *O*bjections, *P*roving, *T*rial closing, *I*nsuring, and *C*losing. Let's deal briefly with each factor.

Objections, as most experienced salespeople have learned, are a normal and useful part of sales interviews. The prospective customer who doesn't offer any resistance to your sales message might not even be listening. The handling of objections—that is, overcoming sales resistance—is so important in any sales presentation that Chapter 5 is entirely devoted to this topic.

For now, keep in mind that objections help you to learn more about the customer's reaction to your message and present attitudes toward your product. Objections should be welcomed enthusiastically as opportunities to uncover more about your customers' needs, wants, and attitudes.

Proving is the factor in OPTIC that becomes necessary when a prospect seems skeptical of the merits of a benefit that you believe to be important to him or her. Proving basically involves using available evidence that substantiates the benefit claims you've already made.

For example, let's assume that you are a carpet salesperson and are in the process of making a sales presentation to a retailer who says to you: "Sure, all that sounds great, but how do I really know this fabric won't fade?

At this point, what the prospect really wants is *proof* of your product claims. You might say something like the following: "Mr Retailer, you've brought up a good point, since no one wants a rug that loses its original luster. As you may know, rugs made of synthetic materials resist fading. In fact, recent research done by *Consumer Reports* compared the fastness of synthetics with that of natural materials and concluded that synthetic materials resist fading five times better than natural fibers. All of our rugs are made with synthetic materials, so you can rest assured that your customers will be satisfied with any of our products that they buy from you."

In general, proof statements are likely to be most effective when they are restatements of a previously mentioned benefit and when they offer credible evidence that substantiates your claims.

Trial closing is the next important element of OPTIC. The expression *trial closing* means an effort by the salesperson any time during the sales presentation to obligate the prospect to purchase a product or service. It's highly important to recognize that closing opportunities might occur *any time* during a sales presentation rather than only at the end of your message.

As a salesperson, you should continually look for **buying signals** that could suggest an opportunity to attempt a close. For example, let's assume that you're with a customer and have barely begun your sales presentation. In fact, so far you've discussed only one of your product's benefits. Your prospect, however—who has already agreed that the benefit you've stressed is useful—seems to believe your product claims. At this point, there's little need to discuss additional benefits or even make proving statements related to the agreed–upon benefit. Instead, merely begin your trial closing efforts.

There are a wide variety of closing techniques; these will be covered in Chapter 7, which is devoted exclusively to the topic of closing. Keep in mind, however, that an important ingredient of any closing efforts is the assumption that you have already made the sale. You might reveal your positive assumptions by saying something like, "Then, Ms. Shure, we've agreed that you need...." If Ms. Shure offers no resistance to your trial closing efforts, then you could begin to write up the order. You might clinch the sale by asking: How would you like to pay for this unit—with cash or on our credit plan?

Insuring, the I segment of OPTIC, is another important element that you might have to employ at any time during a sales interview. To *insure* means to make certain; to reduce, eliminate, or transfer risk. A safe generalization is that most customers don't like to make bad buying decisions. For some buyers, far more than time may be lost. Also at risk can be lost profits, damaged reputations, and bruised self–images.

As a result, you should continually be sensitive to the need for providing information and reassurance showing how the prospect's risks are minimized by purchasing your product. Methods for reducing prospect risk include stressing product quality, explaining warranties, and guarantees, and discussing service and repair facilities.

Closing, that all–important element of OPTIC, significantly influences your future with your company as well as your own standard of living. Closing is the attempt to motivate a customer into making an affirmative decision regarding the purchase of a product or service. In short, the purpose of the close is to get the order. We'll hold off a detailed discussion of the close until a later chapter.

Stare out the window for a moment and try to recall and describe in your own words what the acronym FUN–FAB OPTIC represents.

107

Guidelines for Making Good Presentations

Table 4.2 presents a checklist of essential characteristics of effective sales presentations. Consider each of these factors when you prepare a sales presentation. Can you see how they relate to AIDCA and FUN–FAB OPTIC concepts?

Table 4.2 Guidelines for making effective sales presentations.

Well–planned sales presentations generally should:

- *Arouse and maintain the interest* of the prospect.

- Show how your product or service can *provide a solution* to a specific problem or *satisfy a specific need or want.*

- *Motivate* the prospect into *action.*

- Be *credible.* If you make outlandish claims about your product, you are likely to find your prospect becoming skeptical of you.

- Be *clear.* Speak at an intelligible rate and in terms your prospect will understand. Don't assume that the prospect is familiar with all of your technical jargon.

- Involve *two–way communication.* If you fail to ask questions that will uncover the buyer's needs and don't listen to his or her responses, your presentation may wander down blind alleys.

- Describe the potential *benefits to your customers,* not to you or your company. Most customers do not buy solely because you might win a free trip to the Canary Islands.

- Be *flexible. You* should be able to adapt the presentation to the needs, wants, and interests of the prospect.

- Be as *complete* as is necessary to guide the prospect into making a favorable buying decision.

- *Provide opportunities for trial closes.*

TYPES OF SALES PRESENTATIONS

Companies throughout the world have developed a variety of techniques and approaches for presenting their sales messages. Regardless of the names assigned to them, most planned sales presentations are a variation or a combination of four basic types:

- The standard *memorized* presentation

- The *outlined* presentation

- The *programmed* or *survey* presentation

- The *audiovisual* presentation

Each has its advantages and disadvantages.

The Standard Memorized Presentation

Should a sales presentation ever be memorized? You are likely to find sales managers disagreeing on this point. Some are completely against a canned approach, while others argue that a **standard memorized presentation** ensures that salespeople will deliver the most complete and orderly presentation possible. Still others feel that a partially memorized presentation is helpful, particularly for less experienced salespeople.

The memorized approach is said to have been started back in 1894 by John Patterson, who was then president of the National Cash Register Company. Patterson studied the presentations of his most successful sales representatives and developed what he called a primer, a booklet containing a standard sales presentation. He then required all National Cash Register salespeople to memorize its contents and employ identical presentations in their selling activities. Due to increased sales volume, the results seemed indisputably successful, so other business firms were quick to adopt similar techniques. The assumption was that success would be relatively automatic if all salespeople presented their sales messages the way the more successful salespeople did.

The standard memorized approach is still used extensively in house–to–house ("in–home") selling, in the selling of life insurance, and in combination with other presentations. As already mentioned, less experienced salespeople often find this method useful, at least until they have developed their own styles of presentation. Among the advantages of the standard memorized presentation are that:

- It is often the result of highly planned and proven activities.

- It tends to be complete and is less likely to overlook key points.

- It can be developed to anticipate and overcome typical buyer objections.

- It is helpful for less experienced salespeople.

- It can result in a more orderly, logically flowing presentation.

On the other hand, as already noted, many sales managers discourage the use of a memorized presentation. Their arguments generally are:

- It can seem excessively canned and mechanical, thus coming across as artificial and insincere.

- It can create embarrassing moments for the salesperson who is interrupted. Lines can be forgotten, and—like the young child selling cookies house–to–house—the salesperson may have to start over at the over at the beginning.

- It makes situational selling more difficult to take place, since communication tends to flow in only one direction.
  It is difficult to use when a salesperson is handling many items or fairly complex products.

In short, not everyone agrees on the merits of the memorized approach. If used, it should be employed in a natural, sincere way and allow for flexibility and two–way communication.

When might a standard memorized presentation be useful? What are some of its potential pitfalls?

The Outlined Presentation

Each prospect is a unique being, and a canned or memorized approach sometimes fails to take this factor into account. Some memorization, however, is not only inevitable but also desirable. As you deliver any type of sales message regularly to a large number of prospects, you are likely to develop a particular and consistent pattern of presentation.

A technique that helps to overcome the potential artificiality of pure memorization is the **outlined presentation**. This type of presentation is sometimes partially memorized. One of its major advantages is flexibility. The outlined presentation is typically an outline of key points that can serve as a memory jogger. The outline may be part of a sales aid, can be memorized, or may consist of key words or letters.

Of course, there are both advantages and disadvantages to the outlined presentation. Among its principal advantages are that:

- It allows for a greater two–way flow of communication than the memorized presentation.

- It seems more natural and extemporaneous—less artificial.

- It has greater flexibility, thus allowing for a more direct appeal to the needs and buying motives of a specific prospect.

- It enables getting back on the main subject easier when the salesperson is interrupted by questions or latecomers to the interview.

111

The following are generally considered to be disadvantages of the outlined presentation:

- This technique makes it easy to get sidetracked onto unrelated topics.

- Relevant and key sales points may be inadvertently overlooked.

- The presentation may not be as carefully prepared or as complete as a memorized one.

- It may not fit the personality of the salesperson who has yet to develop skill in extemporaneous speaking.

All of these disadvantages can be overcome with experience and practice, however. Some salespeople rehearse their presentations on video– or audiocassette recorders or in front of managers, selling classes, peers, spouses, and even their pet collie dogs.

The Programmed or Survey Presentation

Another presentation method, which is sometimes used in conjunction with either standard memorized or outlined presentations, is the **programmed or survey presentation**. More than one sales call is typically required for the programmed method. The first call usually requires the salesperson to sell the prospect on the need for an in–depth analysis of his or her problems and needs—both present and future.

After carefully examining and analyzing the prospective customer's specific problems and needs, the salesperson develops a tailormade program or system to fit them. The actual sales presentation usually combines a written proposal containing technical and price information with an oral sales message. These are delivered on second or subsequent visits with the prospect.

112

The programmed method may be highly complex and require a great amount of study and analysis; it may also be simple enough to be prepared by someone in the office manually or on a computer that has been supplied with the necessary information. This technique is often used by people selling office products, insurance, accounting systems, and industrial equipment.

As with any type of presentation, the programmed sales presentation has advantages and disadvantages. Among its principal advantages are that:

- It stresses the buyer's needs because of the investigative nature of the survey.

- It makes the prospect feel you are sincerely interested in his or her problems and needs.

- It can be an impressive and more professional–appearing technique.

Among the major disadvantages of the programmed sales presentation are that:

- It can be costly and time–consuming because of the necessity to delve deeply into the prospect's situation for information.

- It may be distrusted by some prospects because of negative past experience with salespeople who used the survey approach as a gimmick or in an unethical manner.

- Some salespeople may not be qualified or experienced enough to prepare programmed presentations.

How does the survey presentation relate to the standard memorized and outlined types of presentations?

The Audiovisual Presentation

A common method of delivering sales messages to prospective customers is the **audiovisual presentation**. This technique makes use of equipment that either separately or in combination utilizes elements of sight and sound. The equipment ranges in sophistication from relatively simple overhead projectors to highly sophisticated laptop computers and videotape or disc players.

The audiovisual presentation is sometimes referred to as an automated presentation because, in general, the equipment rather than the salesperson relates the product's features and advantages to customer benefits. The key advantages of the audiovisual presentation include the following:

- It tends to hold the prospect's attention without interruptions.

- It delivers what it has to say in a limited amount of time.

- It doesn't miss any major product benefits.

On the other side of the coin, the audiovisual presentation also has some key disadvantages:

- It may not allow for two–way communication until the full message has been delivered.

- It may cause some salespeople to feel subservient to a machine.

- It may develop mechanical problems that can create embarrassing moments for the salesperson.

Because of the extensive use of audiovisual equipment and other types of sales aids by many salespeople today, we'll further examine their nature and use in the following chapter.

Which type of presentation generally allows for more interaction between the salesperson and the prospect, the standard memorized, the audiovisual, or the outlined? Why?

PROBLEMS, PROBLEMS, AND MORE PROBLEMS

A sales manager once asserted, You've got to learn to live with problems. Where there are no problems, there's no business!" There is a certain element of truth in that statement. The creative salesperson has learned, however, that the frequency and intensity of many problems can be reduced with effective planning. Nonetheless, even the best–organized salesperson will occasionally experience difficulties; some are just impossible to avoid.

The following section is intended to guide you through the maze of occasional difficulties experienced by salespeople during the presentation. It is hoped that you will profit by developing a greater awareness of some of the more common ones and will therefore be better able to avoid them. Table 4.3 summarizes the principal types of problems that may develop during sales presentations.

What—Another Interruption?

Interruptions during sales interviews are usually extremely frustrating to the salesperson who is trying to deliver a sales presentation with a reasonable degree of continuity. Most interruptions are cause by *telephone calls,* the *prospect's assistants,* or *other company personnel.*

What can you do to lessen the frequency of interruptions by telephone calls while you are attempting to deliver a sales message to a customer?

A relatively simple solution to the problem of interruptions is to tell your prospect that your presentation will be far more useful and meaningful if it has continuity and then to ask whether the assistant or receptionist could be requested to hold any interruptions for ten minutes or so. Most prospects don't seem to object to such requests, especially if you've established a positive relationship with good rapport during your approach.

Table 4.3 Guidelines for handling major types of problems faced by salespeople during sales presentations.

Type of problem	Recommendation
• Interruptions	*Ask client to hold interruptions. Request that all key people be present.*
• Short on time	*Suggest another meeting.*
• Lack of ample knowledge	*Don't bluff; check on needed information. Follow up with necessary information.*
• Maintaining Interest	*Use established techniques for maintaining interest.*
• Not being understood	*Use language understood by client.*
• Maintaining Control	*Use questions to guide interview*
• The roadblock	*Maintain cordial relations. Try to contact other members of buying center. Write letters to key decision makers.*

Often interruptions are caused by latecomers. Assume you're in the process of delivering a sales presentation and Mr. Oscar Override, the assistant buying manager, enters the room. Oscar, you have learned, shares purchasing authority with your prospect. What do you do? Your solution to the problem depends on how far into the presentation you are. If possible, give Oscar a quick recap and include him in the balance of the sales presentation. Or, if you feel that your original prospect would be bored by restating the initial part of the presentation, you could tell Oscar you'd like an opportunity to drop by his office a bit later with the complete story. The frequency of this sort of problem can be minimized if you request in advance that all key personnel—that is, those who influence buying decisions—be there during the presentation.

The Squeeze Play—Short on Time

Assume you have a well–planned presentation requiring a minimum of 20 minutes to deliver and your customer says, I'm really quite anxious to hear what you have to say, but all I can give you right now is about five minutes. I've got a luncheon appointment with Hattie Hathook, one of our suppliers, at noon. What did you want to talk to me about?

It is inadvisable to try to squeeze a 20–minute presentation into 5, and such a request places you in an awkward and tense position. Usually, when customers indicate they have less time than you need to make an adequate presentation, you would be wise to suggest another meeting—tactfully, of course. You might even offer specific choices of times. But above all, don't lose your composure or temper because you can't deliver your presentation as intended.

Assume that you are a computer salesperson in a retail outlet. *How would you handle a prospective customer who says the following to you.* "Hi, my name is Ziggy Maslow. I run a management consulting firm, and I feel that I have a real need for about three of your laptop personal computers. Quite frankly, I don't know much at all about computers, but I would like some information. Unfortunately, I have only about five minutes before I have to leave to meet someone. Can you help me.

117

The Unknown Answer

Sometimes a customer may ask you a question that you can't answer. Although a salesperson should strive to be well informed, no person can know everything about his or her company and its products. You should never bluff your answer or offer incorrect information. Instead, you are better off if you admit that you don't have the answer to a specific question. You might say something like, Mr. Waxbyrd, that's something that hasn't come up for a while. I want to make sure I give you the right answer to your question, so let me check on it, and I'll let you know first thing in the morning. Will that be all right?

Rather than guess, what should you do when a prospect asks you a question you are unsure of?

To avoid potentially harmful credibility gaps between you and your customer, it's extremely important that you fulfill any commitments you make. Be certain to follow up and give the customer the information as promised.

Sometimes it's easy to make excuses for not following up, especially when you've been busy or preoccupied with other pressures and activities. You might feel, "Aw, he probably didn't expect me to return the information anyhow." But Mr. Waxbyrd just may be waiting anxiously for that information. He may feel that since you made a commitment to him, you intend to fulfill it. As a salesperson, you should develop the habit of following through on your promises; otherwise, your accounts might think, I can't really trust that person. In the future I'm going to deal with a salesperson I can trust.

Table 4.4 Guidelines for maintaining a prospect's attention and interest.

- Keep your presentations to a *reasonable length.* if you have empathy and sensitivity for the feelings of your customers, you should be able to sense when their interst is waning.

- Allow for ample *two–way communication.* Your prospect's interest is more likely to be maintained if he or she is directly involved and actively interacting with your presentation. Ask probing questions. Then, as you listen to the response, you will be helping to create customer involvement.

- Wherever possible, *appeal to the prospects five main senses:* feeling, seeing, smelling, hearing, and tasting.

- Use *audiovisual aids* such as flip charts, graphs, reprints of advertisements in national publications, films, and even the product itself when applicable.

- Use *third–party references* (testimonials). They help to create a more favorable image of your product or service.

- *Sell the sizzle*—not the steak; that is be careful in your choice of words. For example, which sounds better to you, a product that is "flimsy and cheap or one that's "light and economical"?

- Relate your product's features, advantages and benefits to the *needs* and *wants* of the customer.

Maintaining Attention and Interest

An anonymous, albeit sagacious, French philosopher once advised, *"L'esprit peut seulement absorber ce que le posterieur peut endurer."* Freely translated, this means: The mind can only absorb what the rear end can endure! This bit of profundity brings us to another problem faced by salespeople: the problem of maintaining a prospect's attention and interest during the sales presentation. As you recall, these are the first two items that we learned about in our discussion of the AIDCA concept.

What can you do to hold a customer's interest in your story? Examine the guidelines in Table 4.4. They've been useful for many individuals in sales.

Not Being Understood

The common downfall of some salespeople is their assumption that they're being understood when, in reality, they are using jargon that is too technical for their customers. Use language that is clear and understandable. For example, if you are selling computers and are talking to a prospect with scant knowledge of the computers, guard against saying something like, Mr. Rom, this model comes with a CGA color video display, is bundled with Dos 6.0 and the latest version of Wordperfect for Windows. Furthermore, you can easily increase the keyclick volume by merely hitting the control, alternate, and either plus or minus buttons. And you can toggle between full and reduced operating speed by merely hitting the control, alternate, and downward–to–the–right slash buttons." In short, be certain that you are understood. Ask open questions, if necessary, to find out whether your customer really understands you.

How can you discover whether the language you are using during a presentation is too technical for your customer?

120

Maintaining Control of the Interview

Who should control a sales interview? Most sales managers would contend that a good salesperson always controls the interview but allows customers to feel that they are the dominant force. Control is a subtle skill that tends to develop with experience. You can use effectively phrased questions to help guide the interview. Also, you should maintain control of your sales aids so they don't compete for your prospect's attention.

The Gatekeeper

Occasionally, one of the decision makers in a buying center acts as a roadblock in your path to speaking with all relevant decision makers. Often referred to as **gatekeepers**, these are individuals who determine what information is received by key decision makers. They may or may not actually be decision makers themselves; they could be secretaries or assistants to those with buying authority. Gatekeepers can prevent your establishing contact with critically important decision makers. Gatekeepers essentially screen information and decide on their own what is worthy of being passed on to others. They may even suggest that you not meet with other key individuals who ordinarily would be involved with buying decisions.

What can you do when confronted by a roadblock? Losing your temper might be satisfying but not too productive. You should try your best to maintain a cordial relationship with the person, hoping that his or her attitude will become more receptive. Even if the person continues to feel the need to be a roadblock, it is advisable to let other members of the buying center know that you are willing to meet with them. Doing so, however, is not without some risk. You might anger your gatekeeper. Yet, it is unlikely that you would be in any worse situation than you already were; you probably wouldn't have made a sale anyhow without seeing the other key decision makers.

Some salespeople overcome the roadblock created by a gatekeeper by writing sales letters to key people stressing the advantages and benefits of their products. A letter is also sent to the gatekeeper so that he or she will feel included in the communication.

121

What might you do about a gatekeeper who seems to believe that there is no reason for you to make contact with others in a buying center?

In the space limitation of a single chapter, we can barely scratch the surface of the myriad problems and unusual situations that can confront salespeople during their daily activities. With experience and training, you will discover that a pattern seems to develop, with certain situations recurring regularly. Occasionally, however, you may confront new and unique problems that require the use of *situational selling,* a concept explained earlier in this chapter. After any interview you should analyze the way in which it was handled. If you are not pleased with the results, you should develop and practice improved techniques for future use.

These are terms that you should now be familiar with:

- sales presentation
- situational selling
- AIDCA concept
- FUN–FAB OPTIC concept
- advantages
- benefits
- needs
- audiovisual presentation
- gatekeeper

- buying signals
- insuring
- closing
- standard memorized presentation features (canned)
- outlined presentation
- programmed presentation survey
- objections
- proving
- trial closing

NOTE

1. Adapted from Eugene M. Johnson, David L. Kurtz, and Eberhard E. Scheuing, *Sales and Marketing Management*, (New York: McGraw–Hill, 1986), pp. 61–68, having originally appeared in "Planning the Sales Call," *Sales Manager's Bulletin* (January 39, 1980, pp. 4–5.

CHAPTER 5

MAKING EFFECTIVE DEMONSTRATIONS

When you finish this chapter, you should be able to:

- Explain the importance of dramatic product demonstrations.

- List and describe the positive results to be derived from presenting dramatic demonstrations.

- Employ the use of multiple–sense appeals when demonstrating.

- Utilize the typical types of sales aids employed by today's salespeople.

- Demonstrate the use of the major guidelines for delivering effective demonstrations.

- Understand the potential benefits associated with the use of showmanship.

CHAPTER 5

If one picture is worth a thousand words, then one dramatization is probably worth a thousand pictures.

Marvin W. Hempel, Author

The imagination is a marvelous phenomenon. For example, you can be sitting in the privacy of your living room listening to a theatrical presentation on PBS radio and conjure up images in your mind as to the behavior of the actors and their surrounding settings without even seeing any part of them. However, does such a vicarious experience adequately substitute for your actually attending the performance and seeing and hearing it with your own eyes and ears? Probably not. Listening may be enjoyable, but it's not quite like seeing the real thing. There's something missing from your living room experience.

How does this analogy relate to the selling process? Well, salespeople could come across like a theatrical production broadcasting over the radio waves, appealing solely to their customers' sense of hearing, or they, too, can be much more vivid, appealing to the many senses and emotions of customers. The focus of this chapter is on how you—the salesperson—can improve your sales presentations by more vividly displaying the merits of your products through an activity termed the **demonstration**.

Maintaing Customer Satisfaction

Closing the Sale

Overcoming Sales Resistance

Presenting and Demonstrating the Sales Message 5

Approaching Prospective Customers

Finding Qualified Customers (Prospecting)

Figure 5.1 Demonstrating the sales message is another activity in the selling process.

THE IMPORTANCE OF DRAMATIC DEMONSTRATIONS

As a salesperson, you need not be a frustrated actor or "ham." Yet, think about what a good theatrical performance attempts to achieve. Many of its objectives relate to the AIDCA concept, which we discussed in Chapter 3. Actors do not rehearse hour upon hour solely for the sake of playing to the four walls of a theater. They hope to obtain the Attention and Interest of their audiences. They also want their audiences to desire to view the entire performance, have Conviction, or belief, in the credibility of the actors, and even to engage in the Action, or activity, of recommending it to their friends. Thespians, too, utilize the well–established AIDCA technique.

In a positive sense, how does a well–presented sales presentation resemble a theatrical performance?

So if you want to add some life and zest to your sales presentations and get your prospect's attention, interest, desire, conviction, and action, then you, as with the polished performer in a theatrical production, can derive tremendous benefits from including dramatic product demonstrations in your sales presentations. By **dramatizing** and using **showmanship** in your sales presentation, you frequently can turn a potentially insipid presentation into an exciting and attention–getting experience for your customer. The concept of showmanship is discussed later in this chapter.)

POSITIVE RESULTS OF DRAMATIC DEMONSTRATIONS

Whether you sell consumer goods, industrial equipment, or services, there are positive results to be derived from presenting dramatic product demonstrations. Let's briefly examine some of these benefits.

Maintains Attention and Interest

The mind of your customer can think far faster than you can speak. What, then, might your customer's mind be doing while you are delivering a straight verbal presentation? You've guessed it! Unless your prospect has had training in effective listening, there is a good chance that his or her mind will occasionally go "out to lunch." The human mind tends to wander from time to time when it is not actively involved with a conversation. One of the major benefits, therefore, of a dramatic and lively presentation is its tendency to help *maintain the active interest and attention of the prospect for longer periods of time.*

How can dramatic presentations help in maintaining your customer's attention and interest?

Substantiates Sales Claims

Customers, as we know, are often skeptical of sales claims. Probably they have good reason, since they've been exposed to many that were mere puffery. Prospective customers want proof with your statements, and a dramatic visualization of a product can be a highly effective means of substantiating sales claims.

Take, for example, the case of an auto salesperson named Rosie. She can talk and talk and talk about the luxurious quality and outstanding features of the all–new Belchexis automobile. But if Rosie takes her prospect for a demonstration ride and provides the person with an opportunity to feel and drive the vehicle, she'll find that her demonstration will be far more persuasive than any of her verbal claims.

How can a dramatic product demonstration help to overcome the natural skepticism some customers may have toward you?

Appeals to the Senses

Imagine, for the moment, that you are a salesperson of fine leather attaché cases, and one of your customers, Mr. Clint Northwood, is seated behind his desk, his eyes covered with a blindfold. He informs you that his doctor requested him to rest his eyes this way each all day while he recovers from his recent radial keratotomy eye operation. That isn't all. Mr. Northwood also has both hands bandaged as a result of an accident that occurred while he was lighting his gas barbecue last Sunday afternoon. To make matters even worse, he has a dreadful cold, which has significantly affected his senses of smell and taste. Nevertheless, Mr. Northwood advises you: "Don't let my problems get in your way. Go ahead with your presentation."

Can you see how your presentation might be handicapped? You would have lost one of the most effective means for dramatizing your sales message—the use of **multiple–sense appeals**. Unfortunately, many sales talks are presented as though each customer were suffering the same maladies as Mr. Northwood. They lack visual vividness and attention–holding effectiveness. Words alone can be effective, but an appeal to a person's emotions and senses can result in clearer, livelier, and far more meaningful presentations.

Try, if you will, to describe solely with words the tastes and aroma of a thick salmon steak surrounded by steamed brown wild rice. You might be able to come up with a fairly good verbal description, but imagine how much more impact your description would have if your listeners could also see, smell, and taste the steak.

Can you think of three examples illustrating the use of multiple–sense appeals in sales dramatizations?

Makes Selling Points Easier to Understand

The operation of a product that has been dramatically demonstrated is far *easier to understand* than if described only by words. Imagine, for example, how different and much more complex your presentation might appear if given to a person with extreme visual limitations. The combined use of sight and sound almost always has far more impact on the prospect than either medium used alone. By actually showing and demonstrating your product or by utilizing various selling aids, you can take advantage of a customer's senses and make presentations much clearer.

Facilitates Selling of Complex Products and Services

Certain products or services are quite complex and would be far more difficult to sell without the opportunity to creatively dramatize them. For example, one firm provides its salespeople with portable laptop computers that explain the company's complex circuitry in its electronic components in a 5 minute message. This graphic dramatization has proven to be so clear and effective that the usual need for supplementary presentations by

131

engineers was eliminated, thus reducing the firm's selling costs. The point is this: a dramatic presentation can often make demonstrations of complex goods and services *far more meaningful* to the prospective buyer.

Shows How to Use Products

If customers are to be satisfied with your products, they must understand how they function. Another important application of dramatic demonstrations is showing how a product can be used. A dramatization can use the product itself (as when a seller of computer software loads the program into a computer and shows a prospect how it functions), or it can use various types of selling aids.

For example, audio/video systems have been used by the salespeople of medical products companies to dramatize contact lenses. The video equipment is sometimes provided to eye doctors to instruct them on the use of the product and on the proper care of the eyes. In some cases, doctors purchase the audio/video equipment from salespeople but receive the discs free.

How does this statement relate to your demonstrations? "Our best salesperson is our product itself."

Makes Sales Presentations More Orderly

A dramatic sales presentation requires planning and rehearsal. Therefore, giving the customer a dramatic demonstration tends to result in more orderly and better organized presentations. For example, the use of sales portfolios, film transparencies, videos, or other visual materials tends to ensure a consistent presentation regardless of the mood of the salespeople during the interview.

How can the use of selling aids help your overcome your normal ups and downs in moods?

Seven reasons why dramatic demonstrations can help you in your selling efforts are summarized in Table 5.1.

Table 5.1 Reasons why dramatic product demonstrations can assist selling efforts.

- Maintains attention and interest

- Substantiates sales claims

- Appeals to the senses.

- Makes selling points easier to understand

- Facilitates selling of complex products and services

- Shows how to use products

- Makes sales presentations more orderly

THE USE OF SALES AIDS

It has long been said that one picture is equivalent to at least a thousand words. If you subscribe to this old Chinese proverb, then you might agree that you have a lot to gain by not just *telling* prospects something you can also *show* them.

Visual aids, such as flip charts, graphs, and portfolios, and copies of company advertising have been used effectively by salespeople for many years. And an increasing number of companies have begun providing their sales forces with audiovisual aids, such as videocassettes and laser discs, which incorporate both sight and sound into sales presentations.

133

Salespeople sometimes carry copies of current advertisements, called *advertising facsimiles,* with them during sales calls. These items can lend prestige to the salesperson's firm. Facsimile ads can also be used by dealers for promotional tie–ins and as mailers to their own customers.

A medical doctor typically has many types of tools available to help in doing his or her work—examining and treating patients. A salesperson also has many types of tools—visual and audiovisual—to help in doing his or her work—selling. The salesperson, like the doctor, doesn't use every available tool or aid with every client. Both the doctor and the salesperson must use sound judgment to determine which type of aid can perform the desired task most effectively.

New types of aids are continually being developed. Well–organized salespeople continually reevaluate their sales aids to make certain that they are not only up to date but also in good condition. Table 5.2 summarizes the major types of selling aids.

Table 5.2 Major types of selling aids.

• Products	• Portfolios
• Models of products	• Catalogs
• Photos and illustrations	• Kits
• Advertising facsimiles	• Guarantees and warranties
• Charts	• Product data sheets
• Graphs	• Portable audiovisuals

HOW TO DELIVER EFFECTIVE DEMONSTRATIONS

An effective demonstration doesn't just happen; it takes considerable planning, rehearsal, and periodic reevaluation. Demonstrations that have proven to be most successful generally apply the following guidelines cited in Table 5.3. Each factor is briefly discussed below.

Table 5.3 Guidelines for delivering effective demonstrations.

- Be certain that your product or sales aid is in good working order.

- Choose a good setting for the demonstration.

- Recognize the individual nature of each customer.

- Appeal to your prospect's senses.

- Involve the prospect in your demonstration.

- Speak as though your sale depended on it.

- Maintain control over the demonstration and your sales aid.

- Keep your demonstrations fresh, short, and lively.

Be Certain That Your Product or Sales Aid Is in Good Working Order

Something that should go without saying but is ignored so frequently that it must be said anyway is this: *Be certain that the product you intend to demonstrate or the aid you intend to use is in good working order.* Check any equipment *before* demonstrating it in front of your prospect. If you're using an overhead projector, carry a spare bulb with you. A burnout during a presentation can be disconcerting and embarrassing if you aren't prepared for it.

Your products or aids should not only be functioning well but should also look good. We know that salesperson is judged by his or her appearance. The same holds true for equipment or sales aids.

Why should your sales aids be regularly checked and maintained?

Choose a Good Setting for the Demonstration

Related to a well–functioning sales aid is the need for a good environment in which to demonstrate your product or use your sales aids. The product or aid should not be demonstrated in dirty, cluttered, or noisy surroundings—such surroundings will compete for your prospect's attention. Try to choose a place and time where distractions and interruptions will be minimal. If using an aid requiring special facilities, such as electrical outlets or water, be sure in advance that they're available. And keep in mind that the presence of an electrical outlet on a wall does not necessarily mean that electricity is going to flow through it.

What sort of settings might detract from the effectiveness of your product demonstrations?

Recognize the Individual Nature of Each Customer

You should have already learned about the importance of focusing on the specific needs and wants of each prospective buyer when delivering a sales presentation. The same advice holds true for the demonstration, which is an integral part of a good sales presentation. In a sense, you should apply what could be called **situational demonstration**, in recognition of the fact that the type of demonstration that appeals to one prospect will not necessarily appeal to another. Be empathetic and sensitive during your delivery in order to ascertain whether you are gaining the prospect's approval or disfavor.

How does the concept of situational demonstration relate to your presentations?

Appeal to the Senses

As we have learned, a sensory appeal is far more effective than words alone. Wherever possible, appeal to the prospect's senses of touch, sight, taste, smell, and hearing. Assume that you are demonstrating stereo speakers. Using only one compact disk player, you could alternate between two sets of speakers to contrast their differences in quality and sound. The quietness of an automobile engine, the firmness of a mattress, the smell of flowers, the "mouth–watering goodness" of chocolate candy—all of these are examples in which sensory appeal can be used. Use them when possible, for they enable the prospect literally to "feel" your products.

Involve the Prospect in Your Demonstration

When demonstrating your product or using sales aids, always try to determine the effect that the demonstration is having on your customer. Does your prospect appear to be tuned in or, instead, is he or she mentally a long distance away? If the prospect's mind appears to be elsewhere, then perhaps you have not involved her or him enough in your demonstration. Directly involving your customers as much as possible helps to maintain their attention. Such simple things as asking your prospect to plug an electrical selling aid into a wall outlet or turn a switch off or on can help

137

maintain involvement. If you are demonstrating a product, having the prospect try to operate it, or at least help in its operations, can serve not only to involve the individual but also to back up any verbal sales promises you may have made regarding performance. And an important "must": ask regular questions to see whether the demonstration is being understood and accepted by your prospect.

What are some ways in which you can directly involve your customer in your product demonstration?

Speak as Though Your Sale Depended on It

In order to deliver an effective, dramatic presentation, you have to be understood. So why not speak as though your sale depended on it—since it does! Try to avoid monotony in your voice, or you might do any outstanding job of lulling your prospect to sleep. If possible, practice your demonstration with a video camcorder or—better yet—record an *actual* presentation and analyze it later for clarity and understanding.

Don't forget to put inflection and variety in your voice, pausing at choice moments. Vary your pitch where applicable. Also remember to choose your words carefully. Don't sell fried potatoes slices; sell crisp, crunchy, flavorful and fresh potato chips! But don't let your efforts at creative dramatization make you forget why you're really there; *to fulfill the needs and help solve the problems of your customers.*

Maintain Control Over Your Demonstration and Sales Aids

Many salespeople commit the cardinal errors of passing out sales literature at the beginning of their presentations or permitting their prospects to get hold of sales aids. Think about what can happen if you place a brochure or sales aid into the hands of your prospect. He or she may become so engrossed with the aid that your demonstration will receive scant attention.

Visual aids are useful as sales tools, but you should maintain control of them as much as possible. Of course, you don't want to become involved in a childish tug–of-war if your prospect grabs the sales aid out of your hands. Usually a polite remark, such as "I'll be glad to leave this brochure with you, Ms. Brash, but if you don't mind, I'd like to use it in my presentation." The prospect will generally accede to your request.

What tends to happen when you lose control over your sales aids during a presentation?

Keep Your Demonstration Fresh, Short, and Lively

Have you ever heard a sales presentation that sounded as though it had been delivered no less than 5,280 times by the salesperson? An effective demonstration avoids a stale, tired appearance. A key factor in making a demonstration interesting is to keep it fresh and lively, regardless of the number of times you've presented it. If you are showing a video with occasional humorous sections, laugh as though you've heard it only two or three times. Laughter is contagious and will spread to your audience. With practice and genuine enthusiasm, your reaction to any sales aid—regardless of the number of times it has been used—can seem natural, fresh, and sincere.

How do you keep a sales presentation that you've given many times appearing natural, fresh, lively, and sincere?

Sales presentations are often too long, and many attempt to cover too much territory. Discover the needs and desires of your prospect and deliver a presentation that discusses only what is necessary. An excessively long dramatization will not only fail to maintain the prospect's interest but can also hurt your chances for a successful sale.

THE SHOW MUST GO ON! THE USE OF SHOWMANSHIP IN DEMONSTRATIONS

Showmanship has long been used by high–volume salespeople in dramatic presentations. Basically, **showmanship** is the act of vividly and dramatically demonstrating the features, advantages, and benefits of a product or service in unusual ways to acquire and maintain the prospect's attention and interest.

For example, one packaging firm uses a highly dramatic example of showmanship in demonstrating the strength and protective features of one of its products. "Throw this box against the wall...then open" are the instructions on the shipping container holding one fresh egg. The egg is immobilized under a film of transparent plastic that is vacuum–drawn and heat-sealed to the inner surface of the carton. The potential customer opens the carton after pitching it against the wall and then reads a card insert that says, "Unless you have the arm of a major–league pitcher, we're betting our egg is still OK." This is a vivid example of showmanship. The salesperson can involve prospects by letting them throw the carton. Far surpassing the effects of mere words, the unbroken egg is visual proof that the claims of the salesperson are valid.

A Caveat

There are some sales managers who harbor negative feelings about the use of showmanship in sales presentations. They feel that such activities do not convey the sophisticated, businesslike air that clients prefer. Numerous other managers disagree, however, believing that the most effective way to convince a prospect of the merits of products or services is to appeal to as many senses and emotions as possible.

There are also some customers who react negatively to the idea of showmanship, but what they are probably reacting to is behavior that is ostentatious and insincere and not to showmanship per se. However, one prospect may be impressed by your ability to apply showmanship, but another might be distracted or even irritated by the same presentation. A salesperson who utilizes showmanship should tailor the presentation to the particular client. Your presentation should not be presented in an insincere,

140

undignified manner or in any way that would give a bad impression of salesperson, the company, or the product. As with any presentation, showmanship should focus on the needs and wants of the prospective customer.

These are terms that you should now be familiar with:

- demonstration
- dramatizing
- showmanship
- multiple–sense appeals
- visual aids
- sales aids
- situational demonstration

CHAPTER 6

OVERCOMING SALES RESISTANCE

When you finish this chapter, you should be able to:

- Summarize six principal types of buyer objections.

- List and describe twelve techniques for overcoming objections.

- Apply the major techniques for handling objections to given sales situations.

- Contrast open with closed and alternate–choice questions.

- Recognize the importance of maintaining an objections file.

CHAPTER 6

Never treat objections as a "No" answer. All they mean is "not yet."

"A SALES BULLET" Economics Press

An objection in a sales talk is like a small piece of eggshell in an order of soft–boiled eggs. When you run onto the shell, you remove it—and go on with the business at hand.

PERCY H. WHITING

"I can't afford it right now." "I'm really not interested." "The one we have still works okay." "It wouldn't work for us; our needs are different." Statements like these don't surprise experienced salespeople. They know that resistance to their messages—that is, **objections**—are a normal part of the selling process.

As a salesperson, should you feel threatened if prospects resist your sales messages or react negatively to them? Not at all. In fact, prospective buyers who don't offer any resistance may be thinking about a weekend skiing trip instead of listening to your presentation. So don't be afraid of objections— welcome them as opportunities for learning more about the prospect's attitudes toward you, your company, and its products.

Objections can be looked at as opportunities to convert resistance into sales. In fact, long–run success in selling hinges significantly on your ability to turn buyer resistance into sales opportunities. Objections may arise at any time during a sales presentation, and you have to be ready for them. In this chapter we explore some of the proven techniques used for overcoming objections and then examine the more common types of objections you are likely to be faced with as a salesperson.

145

Maintaing Customer Satisfaction

Closing the Sale

Overcoming Sales Resistance 6

Presenting and Demonstrating the Sales Message

Approaching Prospective Customers

Finding Qualified Customers (Prospecting)

Figure 6.1. Overcoming sales resistance is another activity in the selling process.

WHY DO PROSPECTIVE CUSTOMERS RESIST?

Psychologists believe that resisting change is a natural human tendency. For many individuals, the old, familiar methods and products are better or more useful than the new ones, which are sometimes viewed as threatening or less predictable. For example, you may still run into an occasional person who resists utilizing a computer or word processor even though the highly practical tools have been around for more than forty years. As a salesperson, you are the force opposing a prospective customer's desire for stability and certainty. Your goal is to modify the behavior of potential buyers; therefore, every time you persuade them to purchase your products, you are an instrument of change.

The Desire to Be Persuaded

If you could get into the minds of prospective buyers, you might discover that frequently they have a genuine interest in your product, may even have the urge to make a purchase, but want to be convinced, or at least reassured, that their decisions will be right ones. Some objections that appear genuine are, in reality, *indirect requests for more information.* When a prospect says, "I can't afford it," he or she may actually mean, "Tell me why it's worth that price." In some instances, objections are intended to test the salesperson's ability and knowledge. Objections, which are often used by prospects as protective shields, can be persuasively and gently removed by the deft activities of creative salespeople.

What might a prospect really mean when he or she says to you, "I can't afford it"?

Common Types of Resistance

You should attempt to learn the typical types of objections that you are likely to be faced with as a salesperson. By anticipating and preparing for them, you'll discover that you enjoy the experience of overcoming resistance, an activity that can give you strong feelings of personal satisfaction and self-worth. Furthermore, the prospective customer who openly expresses specific objections provides you with a guide to how you should continue

147

your sales presentation. The prospect who says nothing, on the other hand, may also be internalizing objections, which, when kept inside, fail to guide you.

Why should you welcome rather than fear objections?

Let's assume that you've done your homework. You've done an outstanding job of qualifying the prospect in advance and have called on someone who needs (whether recognized or not) your product or service. You are still likely to receive some resistance, objections that typically fall into one of eight principal categories, as summarized in Table 6.1. Understanding these types of objections can help you answer them more skillfully. A little later we'll discuss each of them in detail.

Table 6.1 Typical categories of customer objections.

Common Types of Objections

- Price

- Product

- Waiting for improved technology

- Source and service

- Salesperson

- Poor time to buy

- Inherent suspicion

- Excuses

HOW TO OVERCOME OBJECTIONS

Resistance to any sales message is a somewhat natural tendency. In order to guide a customer into accepting your proposal, you need a tremendous degree of empathy: you must continually try to put yourself into your prospect's shoes. Try to classify your prospect's objections. Ask yourself whether they're genuine or merely a cover–up for other feelings. In developing methods for handling objections, you should carefully consider how to conduct your presentation.

Let's look at some of the techniques regularly used by professional salespeople to overcome objections. (See Figure 6.2 for a graphic summary of the major techniques.)

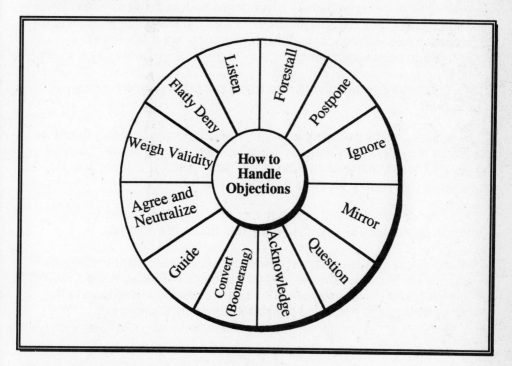

Figure 6.2 Techniques for overcoming objections.

Listen to Objections

Although talking is a necessary ingredient to selling, during the early stages of your sales interview, **listening** is of far greater importance—particularly if you sincerely want to learn about your prospect's needs and attitudes. Effective listening, accompanied by creatively asking questions, helps both you and your prospect. It helps you learn, for example, why your prospect may be resisting your sales message, and it helps the prospect get out into the open any negative feelings he or she might have.

Customers who are listened to are more likely to feel that you have a sincere interest in their needs and problems. When objections are brought out into the open, they frequently seem less real to the prospect. Also, people don't generally like to be contradicted. If you argue with or insult the intelligence of your prospect, you are almost certain to lose the sale–even if you win the argument. Your techniques should subtly guide—not push—your prospects into positive agreement.

Why is listening so significant as a technique for your overcoming objections?

Unfortunately, many salespeople are poor listeners; they feel that they're in control of the sales interview only when talking. Such is not the case, however. Cicero, that ancient Roman statesman seemed to recognize the importance of effective listening when he orated:

God gave us two ears and only one mouth. In view of the way we use them, it is probably a very good thing that this is not reversed.

Attentive listening is important; it allows customers to air their feelings and sentiments. When objections are allowed to come out into the open, instead of being blocked by one–way communication from the salesperson to the prospect, they can be perceived more objectively by the prospect.

Table 6.2 Reasons for developing improved listening habits.

- Most people like to feel important, and being listened to helps them feel that way.

- Customers tend to be more responsive to sales presentations when they know that their opinions and suggestions are listened to.

- Listening can help to uncover small gripes and prevent them from blossoming into big grievances.

- Salespeople who don't get the necessary facts often make poor decisions.

- Salespeople who jump to conclusions lose the respect of their customers.

Customers, of course, are human, and like anyone can be negatively influenced by the pressures of their jobs and personal lives. Quite often what prospects really need is someone who appears willing to listen to their problems and attitudes. If you—the salesperson—can become aware of these needs through careful listening, you will learn much about what is required to sell a product. There are at least five reasons why you should attempt to develop better listening habits, as cited in Table 6.2.

Forestall the Objection

Although objections are not to be feared, the creative salesperson tries to anticipate specific objections and, in effect, answer them, before they arise, an activity known as **forestalling**. By anticipating negative reactions, the salesperson prevents prospects from being put in a position where they feel compelled to defend their objections. Customers don't have to bring up or defend objections that have already been covered to their satisfaction.

151

For example, you may have learned during your pre approach that your prospect, Ms. Schmidt, a buyer for a large janitorial service company, prefers to deal with firms that allow her at least 60 days to pay for purchases. Your company, however, requires payment within 30 days. During your sales presentation, you could forestall her objections to a shorter credit period by saying something like the following:

"Ms. Schmidt, you can see that our supplies are not only of high quality, but are competitively priced, factors certainly of importance to you in your operations. As a businessperson, you realize that one of the ways we are able to offer and maintain reasonable prices is by operating efficiently and using businesslike practices, such as asking our customers for payment within thirty days. We've received few complaints on this policy since, by supplying better products at lower prices, we can help customers increase their profits."

How can you as a salesperson benefit by forestalling objections?

Postpone the Objection

Part of your task as a creative, professional salesperson is to sort out real from stated objections, realizing, of course, that they are not always one and the same. You should not, however, regard any customer's objections as trivial, since to him or her they may be quite genuine and of great significance. In some instances, though, it's better to postpone an objection, at least until you've had an opportunity to offer sufficient evidence of your product's value and its benefits to your customer.

One technique for **postponing** objections is to say, "Ms. Balsham, you've brought up a valid point. I'll be discussing that specific subject later in my presentation. If you don't mind, I'll just go on until then, at which time I think you'll find the answer far more meaningful." (Note the "if you don't mind," in the previous statement. Many salespeople believe that you should not postpone an objection without the customer's permission.

Price is one topic that many salespeople feel should be postponed until value and benefits have been established. When you're involved in a field where repeat customers are desired, selling on the basis of price rather than value can be a costly mistake, even when your prices are generally lower than those of your competitors. Say, for example, that you sell office supplies, including floppy disks for computer disk drives, and your floppies are $5 less expensive per 10–pack than the brand currently purchased by your prospect. If you try to sell the $5 savings, chances are you'll find later that another supplies salesperson took the business away from you, either by stressing quality or maybe even by having a price lower than yours. Instead of price, you should stress the quality and reliability of your disks in relation to the customer's needs.

When might it be a good idea for you to postpone answering a prospect's objections?

Ignore the Objections

A technique for handling objections that some sales managers feel may be dangerous to your selling health if not used with caution is the act of simply **ignoring** the objection. It certainly isn't a method you want to use frequently with the same prospect. Some salespeople use this method when they feel the objections are a bit weak. The salesperson may pass by the objection as though it didn't exist and move immediately on to the next point. However, it wouldn't be advisable to ignore the objection when the prospect restates it, since the restatement probably indicates that the objections is important to the prospect. You could respond to a restated objection with one of the other techniques for handling objections in your selling arsenal.

What is your reaction to this statement? "Some objections are merely lame–brain excuses for not buying. The best technique when confronting flimsy excuses is to ignore them."

Mirror the Objection

Our perception of ourselves sometimes changes when we see our reflections in the mirror. A prospect's resistance, too, may change after it has been reflected back to him or her. Another proven method for overcoming customer skepticism is to engage in what is referred to as the *mirror response,* which is the act of restating to the prospect what you think he or she has just said. **Mirroring** a response clarifies your own understanding and also allows prospects to reconsider their own words. Frequently an objection loses its apparent validity when it has been restated by another person. Ways in which you can phrase the mirror response include: "Mr. Prospect, are you saying that...?" or "If I understand you, you're saying...." or "Then you are concerned about...."

The mirror response may also provide you, the salesperson, with clues as to methods for overcoming the prospect's objections. For example, assume that the prospect states, "I really don't think I can use your product because it won't fit in my office." You might rephrase and mirror the objection with something like: "You mean, Mr. Prospect, that my product appears to be too large to fit in your office?" You should then pause and wait for the prospect to respond. Even if the prospect answers with a "yes" you now can proceed with answers to the objection, such as providing ideas on how the room might be rearranged or a different model be acquired as a solution to the size problem.

In what way does your mirroring an objection tend to soften its impact?

Question the Objection

Questioning objections can also be of considerable benefit in overcoming resistance. For example, assume a prospect says, "Based on what I've been hearing from my associates, I don't feel that I can depend on a regular supply from you people." You might respond with, "I'm certainly concerned about what you're implying. Specifically what have you heard about our shipments?"

In effect, by questioning the prospect, you are asking him or her to move from the general to the specific. When this method is used, especially when it's in conjunction with other techniques, the objection often appears less significant to the prospect.

Occasionally, a salesperson may notice that an account's volume of purchases has declined markedly. The ability to phrase questions effectively can often enable a salesperson to uncover the cause of the problem. Assume that you merely were to ask the customer. "Mr. Gonzales, I notice that your purchases have fallen off substantially in recent months; is there anything wrong?" This technique will frequently elicit a limited response, possibly a hasty and succinct no. There are far more effective ways of phrasing questions that increase the possibility of receiving more complete responses. Questions may be phrased as *open questions, closed questions,* or *alternate–choice questions.* Open questions usually generate better responses than do closed questions.

An *open question* is phrased in such a way that it *cannot* be answered with a simple yes or no. For example, "Ms. Carson, now that you've seen a demonstration of our product, what do you think?" If you ask an open question, exercise patience, and *say nothing until Ms. Carson finally responds*, you will discover more often than not that Ms. Carson will be more likely to express her feelings about the product and provide you with some positive clues as to the effectiveness of your sales presentation.

A *closed question* is phrased in such a way that it *can* be answered by yes or no. For example, "I've shown you how the product works, Ms. Carson, would you like to buy it?" Too frequently the answer will be a flat no. In general, closed questions should be avoided unless you are relatively certain that you'll obtain the desired responses.
Practice formulating questions by using the open–question technique. You may be surprised and pleased with your results. Table 6.3 provides a list of key words that determine whether question is open or closed.

155

Table 6.3 Open and closed questions.

Open	Closed
• Who	• Is
• What	• Do
• When	• Has
• Where	• Can
• Why	• Will
• How	• Shall

The *alternate–choice question is* used by salespeople to get agreement from customers by making it easy for them to choose between two or more alternatives. For example, you could ask, "Which one of the items I showed you seems to fit your requirements better, Ms. Shepherd?" Another example: "Well, Mr. Pappas, do you prefer the suit with the vest or the one without?"

Which tends to elicit a more complete response from your customers—an open question or a closed question? Why? Can you state an example of each?

Let's look at another example of the use of questioning techniques.

Mr. Hitch   (a prospect) I hear that SureCo doesn't pay its insurance claims.

Mr. Overt   (insurance agent for SureCo) SureCo doesn't pay its claims (mirror)? Why do you say that (open–ended question)?

Mr. Hitch   Because I know of a man who had his insurance with SureCo three years and for *no reason* at all he was canceled.

Hr. Overt   For *no* reason at all?

Mr. Hitch   Well, that's what I was told.

Mr. Overt   Is that the primary reason, then, why you feel you wouldn't acquire insurance from SureCo?

Mr. Hitch   Well, yes.

Mr. Overt   Wouldn't you agree, Mr. Hitch, that SureCo is in business to make a profit? We don't make it by *not* selling insurance. Mustn't there have been some good reason for SureCo to decide it no longer wanted to accept premiums from the person you've mentioned (closed type of question with likely affirmative response)?

Of course, you must be careful to avoid appearing as though you were conducting an inquisition with the prospect, which would tend to create a defensive and counterproductive atmosphere. Table 6.4 provides additional examples of questions that could be asked under certain circumstances.[1]

> **Table 6.4** Examples of types of questions that could be asked to overcome buyer resistance.
>
> • "Would you mind telling me why you think my price is high?"
>
> • "Could you tell me by how much we are out of line?"
>
> • "We are usually quite competitive on this model, so I'm surprised that you find us high. Are the quotations you have on the same size machine, Mr. Brown?"

How might your use of the questioning technique reduce a prospective buyer's resistance?

Acknowledge the Objection

A low–key response to sales resistance is **acknowledging** the objection. This relatively soft approach can be used to show your prospect that you feel he or she brought up a logical point. In this manner, you show the person that you understand and sympathize with what was said. You aren't conceding anything, however, but are merely acknowledging you understand the prospect's point of view.

Convert the Objection

A fairly common technique for overcoming objections is the **converting (boomerang)** technique, which involves converting objections into selling features. For example, assume that you work for the KaiCan Aluminum Company, and that your customer, Mr. P.C. Ristantz, has just informed you that his firm is no longer going to use your aluminum products. Mr. Ristantz has explained, "We've decided to discontinue the use of aluminum in our products in favor of other raw materials. We've discovered that we have to reduce the weight of our materials yet maintain strength. I really doubt that any of your products can meet our needs."

Your response could be, "Mr. Ristantz, I can certainly understand your needs for both reduced weight and adequate strength. Here's what we've recently done to overcome the problem. We have broadened our lower gauge limit from 0.020 to 0.008. This has result in a 60 percent potential savings in weight over the 0.020 sheet you presently use. And it doesn't significantly alter the integrity or strength of your particular product. So you can see that our sheet aluminum eliminates your need to switch to raw materials you may not be familiar with. This makes good sense, doesn't it?" (Of course, you would use technical jargon of this nature only with someone who was certain to understand.)

How can you convert objections into selling features?

Guide the Objector

Related to the conversion method is the **guiding** technique of handling objections. This method can be used when the prospect has made both positive *and* negative comments about your product. With this technique, you try to guide your prospect's thoughts toward those parts of your proposal he or she has already agreed with. For example, a prospect might say, "I can see several advantages of your equipment over the items I'm currently leasing, but I'm not sure if it's worth the extra cost." You could ask, "What are some of the advantages of our equipment that you feel would be most helpful to you?" Through the use of the guiding technique, you can focus on the positive aspects of the interview and, in a sense, sidestep the negative portions.

How does the guiding technique overcome your prospective buyer's resistance?

Agree and Neutralize the Objection

A method long used by salespeople when facing objections has been termed the **agreeing and neutralizing** technique. Referred to also as the *yes, but* technique, this method tends to reduce prospects' sales resistance, since the salesperson appears to be agreeing with their responses. The salesperson shows empathy for their points of view, which tends to relax them. At this point, however, the salesperson demonstrates that the objections are actually unfounded.

You must be careful with this technique also, since people generally don't like to be contradicted or proven wrong. If you appear contradictory, your prospect is likely to become defensive and to resist your efforts.

The 3M Corporation recommends that its sales personnel use a modification of the *yes, but* technique. 3M salespeople are advised to drop the "but" and in its place use a *pause*. For example, instead of saying, "I don't blame you for doubting that this procedure will work for you, but Mr. Dent at Arrowhead Graphics...," a salesperson might say, "I don't blame you (pause)....Mr. Dent at Arrowhead Graphics...."

Some salespeople use the word "however" instead of "but," feeling that it's a gentler term. For example, a customer might say, "That's one heck of a lot of money to pay for a car." The automobile salesperson then could say, "You're right. it is a lot of money. However, have you considered the low maintenance, high mileage, and extremely favorable resale price you'll get at trade–in time with this automobile?"

Some salespeople use a modification of the *agree–and–neutralize* technique termed the 3F's method. The F's stand for *feel, felt,* and *found.* Here's an example of the **3F method**:

"I understand completely how you *feel*, Ms. Block. Several people I've talked to in the past *felt* the same way. However, here's what they *found* after they tried. . . ."

How do you feel about the agree–and-neutralize technique for overcoming buyer resistance?

Weigh the Validity of the Objection

Assume that your prospect has made nothing but negative comments about your products. In such cases, you could use the **weighing** technique, a method that involves your listing on one side of a sheet of paper all the disadvantages cited by the prospect and on the other side the advantages. No product is perfect, but a visual comparison that shows how the advantages far outweigh the disadvantages can often overcome customer resistance. (See Table 6.5 for an example of the weighing technique.)

How does the weighing technique aid in overcoming your buyer's resistance?

Table 6.5 A graphic example of the weighing technique for overcoming customer resistance.

Advantages	Disadvantages
1. Lower operating costs	1. Higher initial cost
2. Simpler to operate	2. Heavier weight than competitors' models
3. Higher resale value	
4. Greater flexibility	
5. Compatible with broad line of add–on accessories	
6. Local and dependable service facilities	

You should try to involve the prospect as much as possible with the weighing technique. For example, you might say something like, "Let's list all the reasons against your making a decision today." (Let the prospect list as many as possible without interference.) "Okay, let's now review some of the main reasons favoring your making a decision today." If necessary, you can add to the advantages list by stating, "Would you agree that *(an advantage)* would also be a benefit? Good, now let's count the advantages and disadvantages. Hmmm. It looks like the answer is fairly apparent, doesn't it?"

Flatly, but Politely, Deny the Objection

The **denying** method for handling objections is another technique used by some salespeople. A major problem with this method, however, is that it can appear to be argumentative. The salesperson is hitting the prospect head–on with a contradiction. There are some instances, however, when a direct denial may be called for. For example, if a prospect has accused your company of engaging in unethical practices and you know that the charges are untrue, a definitive and sincere denial is a very convincing response. If the accusation about your company is true, however, your future credibility will be adversely affected by your denial.

What is a major danger inherent your using the direct–denial method for overcoming buyer resistance?

See Table 6.6 for a summary of the major techniques for handling objections.

Table 6.6 Major Techniques for Handling Objections

Technique for handling objections	Purpose of technique	Sample response or explanation
Listening	To enable prospect to air feelings, should be used in conjunction with questioning techniques.	Show interest in prospect's feelings through sincere use of listening responses.
Forestalling	To overcome known objections *before* they are stated by a prospective customer.	"In spite of high interest rates, now is an excellent time to purchase a house. Let me explain why, Mr. Capister."

(Table 6.6 continued)

Technique for handling objections	Purpose of technique	Sample response or explanation
Postponing	To avoid even greater buyer resistance that might result from an immediate response.	"You ask how much it costs? Far less than you might think, Mr. Parsimoni. First permit me to show you how these features can actually reduce the costs of operating your business.
Ignoring	To sidestep a prospect's objections when they appear flimsy and without merit, must be used with caution.	Prospect may later recognize the triviality of the ignored objection.
Mirroring	To clarify your own understanding of the prospect's feelings and to enable prospect to reconsider his orher own words.	"You mean that you don't expect *any* reduction in costs as a result of our proposed equipment installation?"
Questioning	To move prospect's objections from the general to the specific so that the salesperson can understand and deal more effectively with them; relates to the mirror technique.	You feel that this product would be too harsh on delicate fabrics? What types of fabrics did you have in mind, Mr. Synique?
Acknowledging	To show prospect that you understand and sympathize (not necessarily agree) with what he or she has said.	You're right, our prices, like everything else, have gone up again recently.

(Table 6.6 continued)

Technique for handling objections	Purpose of technique	Sample response or explanation
Converting (Boomerang)	To convert an objections into a reason for buying.	"The fact that you say you're too busy is all the more reason why you should hear how this system can save you substantial amounts of time."
Guiding	To support favorable remarks the prospect has made about the product and thus guide the prospect away from negative feelings	Let's return to some of those product benefits we discussed earlier. Which ones seem to be most appealing to you?"
Agreeing and neutralizing	To "disarm" prospects by appearing to recognize the merits of the prospect's objection yet returning to your own position with renewed vigor.	"I agree that it's frustrating when children's plastic swimming pools become brittle and crack apart after one season. However we are now using a manufacturing process that eliminates this problem."
Weighing	To show how advantages of the product outweigh any disadvantages.	Let's weigh the advantages versus the disadvantages of this product and I think you'll then agree that . . ."
Denying	To refute an untrue accusation made by the prospect toward you or your company.	"I'm afraid that someone gave you incorrect information. We have *never* canceled a person's insurance for no reason whatsoever."

164

TYPICAL BUYER OBJECTIONS

After a few years of experience, you might find yourself actually wishing that customers would develop some new and more challenging objections. You might even begin to feel that you've heard the same old patter so often that you can handle it easily with the polished responses you've developed. Earlier we saw that objections generally fall into one or more of eight categories. Let's examine those categories now.

Price Objections

One of the most common objections concerns price. Frequent comments of resistance are: "I can get it cheaper elsewhere." Your price is too high." "I think I'll wait until the price drops." Price objections can often be overcome by proving that your product is worth the price being asked. For example, you might justify price by stressing such features as higher quality of materials, better quality control, improved design, guarantees, service facilities, prestige factors, and by using third-party references. The *agree-and-neutralize* method of overcoming objections could also be put to good use in such cases. For example, you might say something like:

> "Mr. Parsimony, you're absolutely right. Our product isn't cheap. Before we get too hung up on price, however, let's take a look at what you will be getting for your money."

Sometimes when customers complain about price, they really mean that they feel they don't have the money to buy the product. Common excuses related to this feeling are: "I just don't have the money," or "I can't afford it right now, maybe later."

Classifying objections is especially important when the objections are based on price. Is the prospect really telling the truth or merely giving you an excuse because he or she doesn't recognize the need for your product or service? Or is the prospect using price and lack of ample funds as a ploy to get you to lower your price? Some buyers are skilled negotiators and have no intention of paying your asking price.

Additional methods for overcoming price objections include pointing out how the prospect may actually save money as a result of purchasing the product, explaining how little a product actually costs by showing how much it costs per day or per application, or suggesting the use of credit terms. If a prospect wants to postpone buying until the price goes down, you can remind the prospect how projected inflationary trends or international value of the dollar may make purchase of the product even more difficult in the future. Those in real estate sales often mention price trends to counter price objections.

How would you respond to this objection? "Your products are somewhat more expensive than some of the others I've looked at."

Product Objections

Another common type of resistance relates to the *product* itself. You may hear objections such as, "Your product is too new; it hasn't been on the market long enough." You can agree with the prospect that your product is new, but raise the question, "Weren't all of today's well–known products— the radio, television, pocket calculators, compact disk players, and video recorders–previously 'too new'? Newness, Mr. Prospect, should be utilized, not feared." In this case you might also use third–party references, show specific research results, and demonstrate the effectiveness of the product itself.

Let's assume that you've called on a retailer--let's assume that she's a woman--who says that she's satisfied with her present line of products. What might you say? You could ask her to check how many of her present products she had five years ago. There undoubtedly would have been a significant change in the types and brands of products on her shelves. You could point out that she kept up with change in the past and that she'll be able to do so in the future if she obtains your products.

How would you handle some of the following common types of product objections? "I don't like the design." " It doesn't have all the features I want." "I'm overstocked with that type of item." "There's no demand for it."

166

Waiting for Improved Technology

We currently are in a rapidly changing and highly technological era. New models of electronic equipment for both householders and businesses continually appear in the marketplace. People differ in their buying motives. Some individuals like to be on the leading edge of *improved technology* by being among the first to acquire a "new and different" product. Others, on the other hand generally are hesitant to purchase the early models of an item. They frequently contend something like, "I'm sure that by next year there undoubtedly will be newer models available that will be much faster, more efficient, and with substantially more capacity. I'd rather wait for the technological improvements."

The hesitant type of prospect often offers similar comments after the "new and improved" model hits the market, since there certainly could be additional technological improvements made to the product the following year.

As a salesperson, you need to deal with such attitudes and face the challenge of convincing the prospect that there is value in obtaining the product now rather than waiting for improved technology. For example, you might explain to the prospect how much savings in operating costs would have resulted if the product had been acquired a year ago. You can also show the prospect how the savings resulting from greater efficiency is greater than the purchase price of the item.

Some customers prefer to "trade up" their acquisitions before they become obsolete. Perhaps your firm offers customers such opportunities, which can be a method for countering the "improved technology" objection. For example, leasing a product for a specific period of time may be possible. The customer may then have the option of either buying or leasing a new model at the end of the leasing period.

How would you respond to this objection? "I think I'd prefer to wait until the models with the 656–megabit DRAM chips are included with the machines."

167

Source and Service Objections

Another fairly common type of objection relates to the *source and service* facilities of the product. For example, a consumer may resist buying in certain stores because of unfavorable reports about them. Or a person may shy away from a particular brand of automobile because of the way the manufacturer assembles it or the way that dealers service the vehicles. Or a prospect may not be familiar with a particular company or its service facilities and therefore have insufficient confidence in the firm's financial stability, dependability, and so on.

Source and service objections can frequently be forestalled by the salesperson who has ample knowledge of his or her company's operations and accomplishments. Ways of forestalling or overcoming such resistance include discussing the financial capability of your firm as well as its age, size, personnel, policies, and service facilities. Using charts and other visual aids can also be helpful.

For example, one swimming pool salesperson—faced with selling in an industry with a damaged reputation brought on by some unethical or under financed builders—maintains a sales portfolio with tear sheets taken from the Yellow Pages of the local telephone directory. He shows his prospects the names of pool companies that were in the telephone directory ten and five years ago. He then compares those pages with a new directory, which no longer shows many of the earlier pool companies. He uses this technique as a means of stressing that his company—unlike many others—will still be around "tomorrow" in the event a customer has a problem that requires service. He also uses the fact that his company is listed on the New York Stock Exchange as evidence of his firm's "financial strength and stability." In his sales presentations, he stresses, "We're not a here–today, gone–tomorrow type of company. We'll be around in the future for you to sue, if need be."

When you're faced with source or service objections, ask probing questions to find out whether the prospect's feelings are based on fact or rumor. When valid, don't deny them. Instead, try to stress the offsetting benefits of purchasing your products.

How would you respond to this objection? "I like the product, but I don't think it's right for me to buy a product that's not made in America."

Objections to the Salesperson

In some cases, a prospect may refuse to do business with a firm because of a personality clash with a specific *salesperson*. Customers may not always openly reveal their true feelings or sentiments, but such attitudes can often be sensed by the alert salesperson.

If you seem to rub a prospect the wrong way, you might try to find out why and then see what aspects of your personality you could change in order to come across more favorably. Are you behaving in a cocky, over-aggressive manner with the prospective buyer? Does he or she find certain mannerisms objectionable? If you're not certain of the real reasons for the personality clash, ask the prospect point blank. You might say something like:

"Ms. Contraire, I feel that there's something about my style of presentation that bothers you. That's certainly not one of my intentions. Would you mind telling me what it is?"

If all efforts to resolve the personality clash fail, then, rather than lose the account entirely, a technique called the T.O. method might be necessary. The T.O. method means *turning over* a difficult customer to another salesperson. In some instances, of course, the **T.O. method** won't be feasible. Then you'll just have to make the best of what appears to be an unpleasant situation. Typically however, objections are generally not of the salesperson. Instead, customers merely have sincere questions that they want answered. Salespeople should continually remind themselves that they personally are not necessarily the object of the objection.

What can you do about a customer who appears to completely dissatisfied with you and your personality?

169

The Poor-Time-to-Buy Objection

Another common buyer objection relates to timing. This type of objection also is commonly used to "brush off" the seller. Probing to determine the validity of such objections is essential.

Typical *poor-time-to-buy* objections include: "Now isn't the best time." "I have to think it over." "I have to discuss it with my partner (wife, husband, assistant)." "I think I'll wait until the price comes down (or the new models are unveiled, or until I can afford it)." To counter such objections, salespeople who have done their homework can show their customers how costly such delays can be.

Frequently, this type of objection is merely a stall. You might ask the prospect which parts of your discussion require clarification and then review them. Perhaps the prospect didn't understand certain aspects of your sales presentation but doesn't want to appear dumb. Try to make it as easy as possible for the prospect to act now, not at a later time.

What would you say to a customer who remarked, "I believe I'd like to think it over before I make a decision."

Inherent Suspicion

Some objections are psychological—that is, they are related more to the mental attitudes of prospective buyers than to the product, firm, or salesperson. One need only look at the growth of the security industry in the United States to have evidence of what appears to be deteriorating trust and *inherent suspicion* among members of our society. Many homeowners in America install "decorative bars" on their windows and buy guns and expensive electronic detection equipment to fend off unwelcome visitors. Many American citizens have never dared to take leisurely strolls at night. Automobiles are equipped to discourage thieves. Some businesses even employ security personnel disguised as company workers to spy on employees.

It is in this unhealthy atmosphere of distrust, where individuals tend to be apprehensive of all their associates, that today's salesperson must function. Should you be surprised, therefore, to discover that your prospective buyers are suspicious and distrustful of what you are trying to accomplish? Looking your customers directly in the eye and providing them with honest responses helps in overcoming inherent suspicion. It should be stressed, once again, the importance of a sound *approach*, the step in the sales process where you significantly influence the relationship and extent of trust you are likely to receive from customers.

Why shouldn't you take it personally when a customer appears suspicious of you?

Excuses

Some prospect are loaded with excuses as to why they can't make a current buying decision. An important characteristic to identify is the difference between an *excuse* and an *objection*. Gus Kotoulas, professor of selling at Morton College, has this to say about the importance of making the distinction between an excuse and an objection.

I use some strong language to differentiate between an excuse and an objection. I tell my students that an excuse is often an untrue statement, and that they must be able to ferret out the real objection before they can continue their presentation. An example might be when a prospect states,

"I have to talk it over with my wife (husband)." The statement may be true, but it also may be an excuse to extricate him– or herself from the sales presentation.

I tell my students to use the following phrase: "Is that all that's keeping you from buying today?" If the customer says, "yes," I tell the student to call the prospect's bluff and ask, Why don't we call your spouse?" If the prospect's statement was the real objection, he or she will usually go along with the salesperson's request. If it's merely an excuse, the prospect might come up with another excuse. I tell my students to keep asking "Is that all?" and calling the prospect's bluff until they uncover the real objection.

171

As Professor Kotoulas emphasizes, you must get through the excuses and work on the real objections in order to make a successful presentation and sale. However, you should be careful during such efforts to avoid appearing confrontational in the eyes of the customer.

What is the difference between an excuse and an objection?

HOW CAN YOU IMPROVE YOUR TRACK RECORD?

We've covered some of the more common types of objections likely to confront those in the selling field. We've also examined some of the frequently used methods to overcome them. However, there is almost always room for improvement in handling sales resistance, especially for the person relatively new to selling. We'll close this chapter with a brief discussion of two ways in which you can improve your own track record in overcoming objections: *practicing your acquired skills* and *maintaining an objections file.*

Practice! Practice! Practice!

Overcoming objections is a skill that comes only with practice. The following little tale has become somewhat of a classic that helps to illustrate this premise:[3]

A confused–looking young violinist carrying his bass violin in New York City came across a taxi driver and asked, "Can you please give me directions on how I can get to Carnegie Hall?" The driver, without hesitation, quickly responded, "Practice, practice, practice!"

The same can be said for the person who wants to improve his or her sales track record. Techniques of selling and handling resistance must be practiced so that you can learn to use them skillfully. A technique used effectively by many salespeople as a means of honing their skills is called role playing, which is an activity that involves creating a realistic situation and then acting out the various parts.

172

When possible get together with other salespeople or your sales manager and role play the customer and the salesperson's behavior. This form of practicing can closely approximate a real situation and enhance your skills greatly for use when you confront the real thing. IBM marketing representatives are formally put through role–playing situations as a part of their sales training. A typical role–playing session might go something like this:[4]

Actor/customer:	I don't think the system is right for us.
Trainee:	Would you elaborate on your concern for me, Ms. Johnson?
Actor:	Well, I have a concern about the cost of the system. I don't think we are big enough to justify it.
Trainee:	If I understand you correctly, Ms. Johnson, your concern is the cost of the system, more precisely the cost justification. Is that correct?
Actor:	Yes, that's correct.
Trainee:	I can understand your concern, Ms. Johnson. Many of our customers have felt the same way, but on a review of the of the cost justification, they have found that the system is fully justified.

Making videos of your role–playing sessions can likewise be helpful as a means of enabling you to see where you need improvement.

What are some of the benefits associated with role playing your sales presentations?

Maintaining an Objections File

Many creative salespeople keep track of the types of objections they receive on the job. Some salespeople write them on cards and develop answers for them (see Figure 6.3 for a sample form). Well–developed responses can be practiced on co–workers and sales managers, or they can be audio or video taped. Experiment with a variety of methods until the techniques become a basic part of you. Always show sincerity when answering objections. If you can maintain enthusiasm for your job and product—along with a good sense of humor and ethical behavior—you should find that handling objections is one of the most enjoyable activities you'll experience during the selling process.

```
Product:_____    Objection No._____

Type of Customer:_____

          Objection or Question        Appropiate Response

          _____        _____

          _____        _____

          _____        _____

          _____        _____

          _____        _____

          _____        _____

          _____        _____
```

Figure 6.3 Objection/response reference form.

These are terms that you should now be familiar with:

- objections
- listening
- forestalling
- postponing
- ignoring
- mirroring
- questioning
- acknowledging
- converting (boomerang)
- guiding
- agreeing and neutralizing
- 3F's method
- weighing
- denying
- T.O.method
- role playing

NOTES

1. Ed J. Hegarty, "Your Price Is Too High," (Chicago: The Dartnell Corporation, 1977), p. 5.

2. Gus Kotoulas, extracted comments from a previous edition of Stan Kossen's *Creative Selling Today,* (New York: HarperCollins*Publishers*).

3. Stan Kossen, *The Human Side of Organizations, 6th ed.*, (New York: HarperCollins*Publishers*, 1994), Ch. 1.

4. Patricia Sellers, "How IBM Teaches Techies To Sell," *Fortune,* June 6, 1988, pp. 72–73.

CHAPTER 7

CLOSING THE SALE

When you finish this chapter, you should be able to:

- Describe why some salespeople experience difficulty in closing sales.

- Explain the importance of recognizing buying signals.

- Recognize the various types of buying signals that suggest it's time for a trial close.

- Demonstrate the major techniques for closing sales.

- Engage in the types of behavior that result in a smooth post–sales–interview period.

- Explain the purpose of the postcall analysis.

CHAPTER 7

Salespeople who cannot close are not salespeople; they are merely conversationalists.

Charles Roth
Sales Manager

What truly measures a salesperson's skill? The number of prospects seen? The fluency of the sales presentation? The deft manner of handling objections? These and every aspect of the selling process are, of course, essential, but they are of little value unless the salesperson has developed another key skill—the ability to close the sale. The **close** is the attempt by the salesperson to motivate the prospective customer into making an affirmative decision related the purchase of a product or service. This is a scholarly way of saying that *no sale takes place until the salesperson gets the order.*

This chapter discusses reasons why some salespeople experience difficulty with this all–important sales step. It also discusses the need to recognize buying signals and examines some of the proven techniques for closing the sale. The chapter concludes with suggestions for post closing activities.

THE ABC's OF CLOSING

Many years ago, those in the selling field believed that there was one—and only one—right time or psychological moment to close. They felt that if it was missed, the chances of making a sale were nil. Over the years there has been a change of attitude. Today, most sales managers hold the opposite view. They believe that good opportunities for trying a close can come at any time during a sales interview. Some managers even suggest that their salespeople employ the "ABCs of closing"—that is, they should *Always Be Closing.*

179

Evaluate these words: "There is one—and only one—right time during a sales presentation to close. If you muff that opportunity, your chances of making a sale are zilch."

The close can sometimes be practically automatic, as when a young woman runs up to the salesclerk in a sporting goods store and hurriedly exclaims, "Give me a can of Sterling tennis balls—quick!" The salesclerk need not go through a sales pitch on the merits of the product and delay the obviously anxious customer. The close, in this instance, comes at the opening. Other closes may take place at any time during a first or even a subsequent sales interview.

REASONS FOR CLOSING DIFFICULTIES

The close is probably the most important step in the selling process, yet it's the one that seems to be the greatest stumbling block to many salespeople. Some individuals, especially less experienced salespersons, make outstanding presentations and handle objections with consummate skill, but then they fail to recognize those all–important signals that urge them to attempt a trial–close. Salespeople, for a variety of reasons, often dread asking for the order, yet they can't remain salespeople for long unless they overcome this significant obstacle. Most sales managers want more than glib conversationalists on their sales teams.

Maintaing Customer Satisfaction

Closing the Sale 7

Overcoming Sales Resistance

Presenting and Demonstrating the Sales Message

Approaching Prospective Customers

Finding Qualified Customers (Prospecting)

Figure 7.1 Closing activities are an extremely significant part of the selling process.

Why is the close probably the most important step in the sales process?

Let's examine some of the common sense causes of closing failures. Studying them should help you develop useful countermeasures and become a more effective closer. The principal causes of closing failures are listed in Table 7.1.

Table 7.1 Principle causes of closing failures.

- Fear of being turned down.

- One–way communication.

- Lack of training.

- Poor planning

- High–pressure selling.

- Lack of enthusiasm.

Fear of Being Turned Down

Franklin D. Roosevelt once asserted, "We have nothing to fear but fear itself." Nothing could be closer to the truth for individuals in sales, yet it is *fear itself*, mainly the fear of personal rejection, which is a major cause for muffing sales interviews. As with almost everyone else, salespeople don't like to be rebuffed: the word *no* can be unsettling and bruising to a tender ego. Experienced salespeople usually learn that their own attitudes toward their jobs and customers influence how they react to rejection. They realize that no salesperson closes 100 percent of the time. They realize that buyer resistance is a normal part of selling activities. They also realize that they aren't being rejected personally—only the propositions they have made. Improved proficiency in closing activities, which develops with experience, helps to reduce the intensity of a person's natural fears.

As a salesperson, you will sometimes find yourself in a difficult position. You must be *sensitive* to your prospect's needs yet *strong* enough to withstand the continually rebuffs inherent in the selling field. You must convince yourself that you are a competent person, that you have a quality product or service, and that your prospects have the right to flatly say no. You must learn to handle such rejection without becoming negative yourself.

DID YOU KNOW?

Babe Ruth struck out 1,330 times, but he also hit 714 home runs.

English novelist, John Creasey, got 753 rejection slips before he published 564 books.

Some salespeople also fear that their attempts to close may seem pushy. Naturally, you want to avoid such an appearance, but if you have an air of confidence, have answered the customer's objections satisfactorily, and enthusiastically believe in your product or service, there is no reason why you cannot be an effective closer.

How might you overcome your fear of attempting the close?

One–Way communication

Another cause of failure in closing frequently develops when the salesperson talks excessively during the presentation. Closing ratios tend to be far lower for the salesperson who fails to ask probing questions, doesn't listen, and isn't alert to buying signals from the prospect. A presentation that is primarily one–way doesn't allow for interaction with the prospect. You should continually be alert, listening to and observing clues that indicate a trial close is in order. There will be more on buying signals later in this chapter.

What does one–way communication lack?

Lack of Training

Successful closes require knowledge, training, and practice. Unfortunately, some individuals in sales have never studied the closing techniques that have long been employed by other, highly creative salespeople. Learn the proven closing methods; then, *practice, practice* and *practice* again. Recognize the typical customer buying signals. Learn how to obtain a series of agreements throughout your presentation. With increased experience and experimentation, you should discover that closing becomes one of the most challenging and satisfying steps in the selling process.

Poor Planning

The close, as with all the steps in the selling process, is merely a link in the chain of activities leading to obtaining an order. The strength of your closing attempts, therefore, will be highly dependent on how well you plan all of your sales activities. Do you qualify your prospect? Is your approach made under favorable circumstances? Do you probe for customer needs, wants, and problems? Do you anticipate how your product could help to satisfy such needs and resolve your prospect's problems? There tends to be a direct relationship between effective planning and a high closing ratio.

How can you best plan for success in sales?

High–Pressure Selling

If you were taking a tour through the Rijks Museum in Amsterdam, how would you like the tour leader to conduct your visit? As you stopped to appreciate the masterpieces of some of the greatest artists the world has ever known, such as Rembrandt, Vermeer, and Frans Hals, would you like the leader to place her hands forcefully on your back, push roughly, and snap, "Let's keep moving; we've got a lot of paintings to see, and we have to be back at the bus by 2 P.M.!"

184

Most tourists prefer a more comfortable pace, one where they don't feel pushed. In short, they prefer being *guided,* not *goaded.* Wouldn't the same apply to customer attitudes? The creative salesperson *guides* prospects—not through museums, but easily and as comfortably as possible through the process of making buying decisions. High–pressure closing techniques generally have counterproductive results. Selling authority George Lumsden warns against the use of pressure when a prospect hesitates to buy. He states:[1]

> Hesitations aren't refusals. Put pressure on a hesitation, and you're likely to get some back pressure. Nudge it a little, and you're likely to get agreement. And it's agreement that closing is all about!

What are your likely results from high-pressure selling?

Lack of Enthusiasm

Enthusiasm is believed by many sales managers to be by far the biggest single factor in successful selling. Naturally, no single factor will ensure success, but an enthusiastic attitude tends to influence customers in a positive manner. Prospects who see salespeople exuding genuine enthusiasm in their presentations tend to develop more positive feelings about the products. It is the lack of this trait that often costs salespeople closing opportunities An enthusiastic manner, however, tends to put prospects more in the mood to make affirmative buying decisions. Enthusiasm, in effect, is infectious and tends to make the salesperson's job much easier. Prospects have more difficulty feeling confident about buying your products or services if you don't appear to be excited about them.

Why is enthusiasm such an important characteristic for you to have?

RECOGNIZE BUYING SIGNALS

A **buying signal** is an *expression, either physical or verbal, of a prospect's desire to make a buying decision.* It may be as subtle as taking off one's eyeglasses and sitting back in a chair or as obvious as the statement, "When can you make the delivery on these items?"

Because buying signals don't always jump out at you, you must be continually attentive to the buyer's body language, comments, and questions. A good time to make a trial close is whenever you see what appears to be a buying signal. Don't be afraid. You haven't made the sale yet anyway, so you have far more to gain than to lose by attempting a close.

Questions as Buying Signals

Buying signals, as already indicated, can be physical or verbal. Watch out for them. Here are some specific examples of questions a prospect might ask that could be a clue for you to attempt a close:

- "Could I try it out one more time?"
- "Is it available in blue?"

- "How soon can I get delivery?"
- "What sort of credit terms can I get."

- "Would you consider my old one as a trade–in?"
- "What sort of a guarantee do you offer?"

- "Is it available without accessories?"
- "Should we move to the dining–room table where we'll have more room to work."

- "Could I please take a look at the contract?"
- "When would you need layout plans?"

186

Statements as Buying Signals

Sometimes a buying signal is more subtle than the listed queries and may be couched in statements like the following:

- "That really looks good."

- "I guess I can afford it."

- "These leather seats are really comfortable."

- "I've always wanted one like this."

- "A friend of mine has one of these, and he says you can't beat it for dependability and economy."

- "Yes, I think it could work for me."

- "It's okay with me; what do you think, dear?"

- "My accountant has recommended a plan like that."

- "Shipment must be complete in 15 months."

- "Our engineers want to approve revisions."

Body Language as Buying Signals

"Your lips tell me no no, but there's yes yes in your eyes," are the insightful words of a "golden oldie" of the distant musical past. These lyrics significantly relate to your activities as a salesperson in attempting to close a sale. Customers don't always say precisely what they mean. They may tell you, for example, that a purchase is out of the question--that they can't

187

afford the product. However, their nonverbal expressions, the message of their eyes and facial muscles or the motions they make (or sometimes don't make) with their bodies may communicate a different meaning. **Body language**, therefore, is another important area for salespeople to understand. Interest in making a purchase may exist when:

- The prospect shows signs of agreement by nodding.

- The prospect's facial expression changes to one of greater receptivity.

- The prospect takes off his or her glasses and leans back comfortably in a chair.

- The prospect appears generally to be more relaxed and intent on hearing your message.

- The prospect intently studies the samples or sales material.

- The prospect performs calculations on scratch paper.

- The prospect pulls out a checkbook or credit card (not very subtle, but a sure sign that you should close!).

Buying signals, as you can see, are not always too apparent. Far more obvious is the need for you to attempt to close sales when buying signals aren't apparent. Let's examine some of the commonly used techniques for closing sales.

Can you think of any other forms of body language not mentioned above that could be considered buying signals?

188

TYPES OF CLOSING TECHNIQUES

Experienced salespeople are usually familiar with a variety of closing techniques, which, in essence, are merely different ways of asking for the order. We can't stress too often the necessity of not being afraid to try to close. After all, since your prospect knows you are a salesperson, should he or she be surprised when you try to sell your products?

We are now going to examine some of the best–known closing techniques. Look first at the major closing techniques in Table 7.1.

Table 7.2 Summary of major closing techniques.

Closing technique	Activity	Sample statement
Positive-assumption close	Assume the sale is a sure thing.	"Please put your name right here where I've indicated with an "X".
Alternate-choice close	Provide a choicebetween two positive alternatives.	"Will this be cash or charge?"
Open-question-and-pause close	Ask a question and wait for the answer.	"How do you feel about this proposal?" (pause)
Multiple-acceptance close	Obtain a series of agreements leading to a final close.	"Then you like the way this car handles? And you say you like a lighter color? Then you prefer only an FM radio? How much of a down-payment would you like to make?"
Minor-point close	Obtain agreement on a minor point to check receptiveness of prospect.	"As you've indicated, you could move in by the first of the month. Is that correct?"

(Table 7.2 continued)

Closing technique	Activity	Sample statement
Contingency close	Make a promise on a promise.	"If I can get the color you prefer by Wednesday, then do we have a deal?"
Future-event close	Suggest buying now before something unfavorable occurs.	"An order placed before the fifteenth of this month will avoid the impending price increase and save you 10 percent?"
Special-offer close	Provide an added inducement to buy.	"We'll give you a free carwash with every purchase of 10 gallons or more."
Trial-order close	Ask the prospect to test the product with little risk.	"Why don't you try this computer in your office for two weeks and then decide."
Suggestion close	Relate to previous point that suggested a purchase should be made.	"Based on the problem you've been having with the service. I'd like to suggest that you try us and I think you'll notice the difference right away."
Counselor close	Advise customer what to buy.	"What we'll do is place some of these items at eye level so that shoppers can see them right away."
Last-chance close (SRO)	Use when supply is limited.	"This is the last time we'll be able to offer it at this price."
Summarize-the-benefits close	Review features, advantages, and benefits related to prospect's needs.	"Coupled with social security, this plan will provide you with the income you and your spouse will need during your retirement."

(Table 7.2 continued)

Closing technique	Activity	Sample statement
Direct-request close	Ask for the order.	"How many cases do you need?"
By-the-way close	Appear to have "given-up", then try one more close.	"By the way, I just remembered that this is the last year you can obtain a tax credit on purchases of this nature. Would'nt you like to save something on taxes this year?"

Assume the Sale

Of all the closing techniques, the one referred to as the **positive close** is the most basic and should be incorporated into all your selling activities. When using this technique, you're simply assuming that your prospect wants to buy your goods. You maintain a positive attitude, one that assumes a purchase is virtually a foregone conclusion. This attitude is easy if you've done your preliminary homework. Let's assume that you have. Then you already know That the person is a qualified prospect. You also know that a need or want exists. Furthermore, you've shown your prospect how you and your products can satisfy these desires, so what's stopping you? Now is the time to assume! If not yet ready to buy, your prospect will let you know. Little is to be lost if you assume, in a tactful and non pressured fashion, that your customer is ready to purchase your product. As a creative salesperson, you have plenty of sales ammunition in reserve, so you're not likely to lose the battle.

The following short conte helps to illustrate what happens when a person fails to use the positive-assumption close:

Jeremy Dussen from Denver drove his car to Albuquerque on a business trip. Uncertain of the parking regulations in Albuquerque, he asked a passing law enforcement officer if he could park where he was. The law

191

enforcement officer said no. So Jeremy asked, "What about all these other cars that are parked here?" The law enforcement officer shrugged, "They didn't ask."

You can use the positive–assumption close by asking such questions as, "Will this be cash or charge?" or "Would you care to have it delivered?" Your choice of words should avoid the use of "I" whenever possible and should convey the impression that an order for your product is virtually understood.

Are you considered to be high-pressured when you assume an affirmative buying decision has been made before your prospect has actually agreed to buy your product or service.

A word of caution: Be alert to appearing to exert pressure with this or any of the closing techniques to be discussed. If the prospect seems upset by your efforts, modify them along softer lines. Some of the following methods can appear high–pressured if your prospect has not been convinced of your product's benefits.

Give More Than One Choice

An excellent way of attempting a trial close is to assume that your prospect is sold on your product or service and then ask a question that calls for a choice. This method, referred to as the **alternate-choice close**, gives the prospect a choice between something and something, not something and nothing. When used, this technique enables you to know immediately whether you've made a sale or if, instead, you must provide additional proof of how the product's features can benefit the prospect. Examples of this close include: "Shall we start with one dozen or two?" and "Will you need delivery by Monday, or would Wednesday be all right?

If you were to ask, "Do you wish to buy this car?" it would be quite easy for your prospect to respond with a flat no. But by asking, "Which model seems to fit your needs better, the two-door or the four-door? you are providing your prospect with the opportunity to make a positive choice between two alternatives.

Why should you give the prospect a choice between something and something than between something and nothing?

Some salespeople misuse this method by giving the prospect too many choices. For example, one computer manufacturer currently offers eleven different models of its portable computer. Any prospect relatively new to the computing field who was given a detailed explanation and demonstration of all eleven computers would probably say, "Er...thanks a lot for explaining all those models to me. I'd better think it over for a while." A better technique is to first uncover your prospect's needs or wants, and then narrow the choices down to a reasonable number—say, two or three models at the most.

Ask an Open Question and . . . Pause

Another method for determining whether or not your customer is ready to buy is the **open–question–and–pause close**. Assume that you have converted the major features and advantages of your products into benefits related to your prospect's needs. However,
you're not quite certain as to your prospect's willingness to buy. By asking an open question and then waiting--and *waiting part is especially important-*-you can often discover whether the prospect is ready to make a purchase. You might ask something like, "Bill, you've seen what this product can do. What are your reactions?"

You can also use this method in conjunction with the forced-choice technique. For example, you could say, "Mr. Fernhopper, you and I have examined your needs and have looked at two models of our palmtop computer, the model SX4000 has a built-in hard disk with a capacity of 30 Megabytes and 2 Megabytes of random access memory, and the model SK 5000 Plus with a capacity of 100 Megabytes and 8 Megabytes of random access memory. Which of these two models do you feel suits your computing needs and desires better?"

In effect, what you are doing with this method is placing the responsibility for making a buying decision squarely on the shoulders of the prospect.

When you use the open-question-and-pause technique, *it is essential that you remain silent and wait for your prospect to make the first statement.* To you, 20 seconds of silence may seem like 20 minutes. To the prospect, the pause provides him or her the opportunity to formulate an answer. If you interrupt the prospect's train of thought instead of waiting silently for a response, you may fail in your closing attempt.

What is a key element to consider when you use the open-question-and-pause closing technique?

Obtain a Series of Acceptances

Another technique that helps in securing an order is called the **multiple-acceptance close**. This involves asking the customer a series of questions likely to elicit favorable responses. When this method is used, the buyer is guided along a receptive path that makes answering the big question—your asking for the order--far easier. Here is an example of how a "paper-flow analyst" for an office machines company might employ the "multiple yes" technique:

Salesperson	Have you every noticed that there are only eight hours in a business day but a lot more than eight hours of work?
Prospect	Yes, I sure have.
Salesperson	Would you agree, as have many of our customers, that paper handling has been an activity taking a disproportionate share of those eight hours?
Prospect	Yes, I would say so.
Salesperson	If I could show you how to turn our paper handling into a process we call "paper-flow," thus freeing people in your office to do more important work and reducing your costs, would you be interested?
Prospect	Of course.

194

What are some psychological advantages likely to result from your obtaining a series of acceptances during a sales presentation?

Agree on a Minor Point

A modification of the multiple–acceptance close is the **minor–point close**. Salespeople who employ the minor–point method try to get agreement on a relatively minor point, which can indicate whether or not the prospect is willing to make the major decision--the purchase. For example, a person selling earth moving construction equipment might state, "Based on what you've told me about your current financial situation, Mr. Cornfield, you would probably prefer to lease rather than make an outright purchase. Is that correct? An agreement from Mr. Cornfield could be an indication that he is ready to buy. Other types of statements implying agreement on a minor point could start with: "We've agreed...." or "As we've seen...." or "As you've indicated...."

The minor-point close seems to be especially effective with prospects who tend to be indecisive--those who feel more comfortable making smaller decisions.

On what type of customer might you use the minor-point close most effectively?

If I Can...Will You Agree...?

A technique called the **contingency close** is involved when the salesperson agrees to do something provided the prospect agrees to make a purchase. This method is especially useful for the customer who is having difficulty making a buying decision. An example of this close is, "If I can get the color and model you prefer, do we have a deal?" Another example is, "I know that time is important to you during the current holiday season, Ms. Dior. If I promise to get the materials to you by next Tuesday, will you place the order now?"

On what type of customer might you use the contingency close most effectively?

195

Order Now Before It's Too Late!

The **future–event close** is a technique that can be used in a variety of situations. Basically, it motivates customers to buy now in order to avoid the greater losses that might, in the future, result from the postponement of purchases. This technique relates to specific impending events. For example, shortages of certain products could develop due to strikes, political activities, international conflict, or bad weather. Or prices may be expected to rise rapidly during inflationary periods or when the dollar is declining on international monetary markets. Salespeople might use the future-event close by saying something like, "With the rapidly deteriorating political relationship between our country and Checkmatania, we don't know how much longer we're going to be able to supply you with our line of imported hand-carved ferndock spreaders. So I would suggest that you stock up now to prevent your being caught short over the Easter holidays." Of course, comments must be truthful, or you're likely to ultimately lose far more than you'll gain.

Why might the future–event close motivate your prospect into buying rather than postponing purchases?

The Special–Offer Close

Salespeople must remember that they are hired to sell--not give--their products away. A tendency of less experienced salespeople, especially when they're confronted with difficult prospects, is to offer to reduce their prices or to let the prospects try a product for a period of time without charge. In general most firms feel that salespeople should avoid giving away merchandise unless doing so is virtually certain to result in greater profits.

There are situations, however, when it is simply sound business practice to make certain concessions to customers. A technique referred to as the **special–offer close** is based on this thinking. It involves providing the customer with an added inducement to make a purchase.

196

The special offer may take a variety of forms. It may be a *sharing of costs,* as when a manufacturer offers to share advertising expenses with retailers for certain periods if the retailers purchase minimum amounts of merchandise. Sometimes the special offer may be in the form of an outright gift, or it may be in the form of special discounts for purchases over a certain amount, or it may be tied in with purchases, as when a chemical firm representative makes the following special offer:

"Harry, let's place an order for twenty–five liters. We'll ship twenty-six to you. You use the first bottle free, and if you're not satisfied, return the remaining twenty–five to us for full credit.

You should, nevertheless, be careful about offering special concessions. Some shrewd buyers never plan to accept original prices. Instead they haggle and bargain, acting as though no deal is possible without reduced prices. In reality, however, they price-haggling approach may merely be a ploy. After all, a prospective buyer has nothing to lose by trying to get a special deal. The astute salesperson, however, should be alert to customers who want something for nothing. A final warning on special offers: you could be breaking the law if you make certain concessions, since there are price statutes designed to eliminate price discrimination and unfair competition in marketing.

Why Don't You Try This for Size?

A closing technique related to the special–offer method is the **trial-order close**. Sometimes used when all else has failed, it involves asking the customer to test the product on a limited scale. For example, you might encourage your prospect to place an order for a quantity far less than your usual minimum order. You can point out how your prospect has risked little, and, if pleased with the product, can later place a larger order.

Sometimes there is no charge for the trial order. For example, a fax machine or other article of office equipment may be lent to a prospect for a trial period with the proviso that, if satisfied, the prospect will order a specified number of the items.

What are some potential dangers associated with your use of the special-offer and the trial-order closes?

Based on...I'd Like to Suggest. . .

Another form of close designed to gently nudge the prospect into making a positive buying decision uses the key words, "Based on...I'd like to suggest...." With this technique you refer to a point previously discussed by you or your prospect and then suggest--based on that point--that the prospect place an order. You can use the **suggestion close** in conjunction with a third–party reference and say something like:

"Harley, *based on* the outstanding success that Major Motors has been having with our components, *I'd like to suggest* that you start with 50 X3Cs."

Here's another example of this method:

"Jenny, based on the enthusiasm you and all of our accounts have shown for our new fall line, I'd like to suggest that you place an order for 150 dresses, which should enable you to have an adequate stock to carry you right through the back–to–school season.".

Can you think of an example of the use of the suggestion close?

Be a Counselor

Once you have developed a sound, trusting relationship with your customers, you will find that they tend to look to you for assistance and advise. After you have earned their respect, one close that can be used beneficially is the **counselor close**, which simply advises the customer how and what to buy.

Assume, for example, that you are a travel agent who has been discussing vacation plans with a prospective client. You might counsel as follows: "In view of your desire to be completely free during your Tahitian vacation, we're going to book you on our package based on a completely new

198

concept of Sea Island Travel. We'll provide you with a round-trip air ticket and a packet of prepaid hotel vouchers covering the number of nights you choose to stay in the French Polynesia. We'll arrange your first night's hotel reservation and provide on-the-spot orientation. After that, you're completely on your own to island hop where and when you want. If you need help, we have consultation service available to you on the islands. Unless you have further questions, I'll book you on this plan. Which have you decided on--the 8-day or the 13-day plan?

Did you notice that more than one technique was combined in the above example? Can you spot the positive assumption, the multiple-yes, and the "based on..." closes blended with the counselor close?

What ingredient is essential for your use of the counselor closing technique to be effective?

Only One Left.

Have you ever noticed how intensely you wanted something you couldn't have? Have you also sometimes felt you would like to have an item owned by someone else? Our next closing technique relates to the these natural feelings. It's termed the **last–chance** or **SRO** (*standing room only*) **close** This close involves an honest statement made by the salesperson as to why the customer should buy now. If the purchase is delayed, the item may not be available later. Real estate salespeople use this technique when there are only a few houses left in a new development. Automobile salespeople also use the SRO method, especially when closing out last year's models just before the new ones are introduced. They might say something like:

"We have only a few of these models left. When they're closed out, you'll only be able to obtain the new model, and at a much higher price. To save money, I'd advise you to pick up one of these while you can."

Don't misuse the last-chance technique, as have some disreputable salespeople who implied that there was only one of an item available when his company had shelves packed with them. You will open gigantic credibility gaps between you and your customers if you use this technique unethically.

199

Why might some prospects distrust your use of the last-chance (SRO) close?

Summarize the Benefits

Some sales trainers believe that among the most effective ways to close a sale is to **summarize the benefits**, especially those relating to features that seem important to the prospect. Some salespeople refer to this method as "summarizing the bennies."

The summary close can be incorporated into most sales presentations. In it you relate the key features of your product to the buying needs of your prospect. This method not only reminds the prospect of the product's desirable features but also helps the salesperson to see whether any additional information needs to be covered. When summarizing, you should avoid discussing benefits not previously agreed upon. If you don't you might find yourself having to overcome new objections. Focus, instead, on the benefits that most attracted your prospect's interests. Don't bring up previous objections. Merely guide the prospect into making a positive buying decision by blending your summary of benefits with one of the other closing techniques already discussed.

Why, when summarizing benefits, should you focus on those that seem to appeal to your prospect?

Why Not Merely Ask for the Order

Another technique for closing, so obvious that many people overlook it, is the **direct–request close**, which simply asks the prospect for the order. Sometimes an outright "May I have your order?" will be sufficient to nudge the prospect into buying. This technique can be especially useful if there is a relationship of trust between your prospect and you. The prospect may have already made up his or her mind to buy but not yet decided on when to place the order. Some salespeople, as already mentioned, hesitate to ask for an order. A more positive and direct method would be to assume that your prospect wants your product and ask directly for the order: "Clarence, how many boxes do you want us to ship?

Should you ever directly ask for the order?

By–the–Way Close

There may be times when a prospect strongly resists any attempts by you to close. A technique used successfully by some people to overcome such resistance is called the **by-the-way-close**. With this technique you give the impression of having given up attempting to make the sale, which tends to relax the highly reluctant prospect. As you begin to leave, you casually pause and then mention another benefit or an old one described differently. You then attempt once again to close. You could say something like.

> (Moving toward the door.) "By the way, Mr. Duro, I just recalled that the new investment tax credit statute enables you to write of 100 percent of the purchase price during the first year. How would you feel about letting Uncle Sam pay a good portion of your investment?"

You have little to lose by attempting the by-the-way technique, since your opportunity to close the deal during the visit with the prospect would have been finished anyway--at least for now—once you went out the door.

What could be a danger associated with your use of the by–the–way close?

Practice Makes Performance

Obviously, you can't use every type of close in every sales situation. And perhaps the list of closing techniques seems a bit overwhelming. If so, study and practice only two or three of them until they seem natural and a part of you. Then, test them in real selling situations. After you've mastered these, learn a few more, try them out, and see which methods work best for you. Continue learning new techniques until you discover those with which you feel most comfortable. Any of the methods could be useful under certain circumstances--another good reason to apply *situational selling* when attempting a close. A technique that works effectively with one prospect might result in a disaster with another. Attempt to know the personalities of your prospects and then select the closing technique that fits each prospect.

201

THE CRITICAL POST–SALE INTERVIEW PERIOD

Once you've convinced your prospect of the need for your product, you ordinarily don't merely utter a magical word or two and disappear from the premises. In fact, your behavior after the close is important from the standpoint of the image you create for your self and for your firm. In most instances, the selling process isn't complete merely because the customer has stated that he or she will buy your product or service. Regardless of your customer's previous feelings your company, your actions at the time of your departure and thereafter will significantly influence your long-run success and that of your firm.

The **departure**, that is the process of leaving the customer's premises, is sometimes a surprisingly awkward activity. If a sale has been made, you may feel either excessive excitement or even an anticlimactic letdown. If a sale hasn't been made, you might feel discouraged and despondent. In either case--sale or no sale--your behavior at this stage is important from the standpoint of yourself and your firm. Remember that sales are frequently not closed during the first interview. Let's now look at some of ideas that can help you with your post interview activities.

Why is the post purchase period, in some respects, as important as your closing the sale?

Don't Dig Yourself into a Post Hole

Tensions are normal emotional reactions for salespeople to feel during sales presentations. A successful sale, accompanied by a sudden release of tension, can sometimes result in weird behavior on the part of some salespeople. To illustrate, assume that you are relatively inexperienced in the sales field. You have just completed a sales presentation and obtained a fairly sizable order. You may suddenly feel so ecstatic over your success and thankful the interview is over that your emotions are about ready to run wild. Now, however, is *not* the time to lose control. If you do, you could lose the sale. Although you certainly should show gratitude and appreciation for the purchase, don't let your emotions get out of control.

Try to retain the appearance of a competent salesperson, one who is accustomed to closing sales. Behaving in a semihysterical fashion is likely to cause your customers to lose confidence in you as a sales person.

Use Your Closing Materials with Prudence

After your customer has agreed to buy from you, be certain you've taken the order correctly. Don't place your trust in memory. It's easy to forget specific items or colors in the hustle and bustle of a busy day. Put all relevant information in writing. Where applicable, get the buyer's signature determine credit arrangements. Something that seems routine but that can actually frighten some prospects is using a pen. Don't whip out your pen as thought it were a concealed weapon. Have your pen and order form out in the open during the entire presentation so that they don't suddenly appear like an invading force from outer space. Some firms help in this respect by supplying order forms that are both sales aids and order blanks. Your pen, too can be a sales aid during your presentation. You can, for example, use it to point to parts of a diagram in a sales portfolio or to key points in testimonial letters.

Reassure the Buyer

Depending on the purchase, many buyers develop certain attitudes after their purchases. They frequently question the wisdom of their decisions, especially those related to more expensive non routine purchases. Your customer, who has just made an important decision, is also likely to have some uncertainties about his or her decision. This feeling of doubt is sometimes called **buyer's remorse**. The post closing period is a time when you can reassure your buyers, informing them that they have made wise choices. In doing so, however, be both sincere and cautious. You don't want to dig yourself into a post closing hole that might cause the customer to reconsider.

A Quick Departure?

Some salespeople believe that the *least* said after a sale has been made the *better*. They feel that many good deals have fallen through because a salesperson became over talkative when he or she thought the sale was final. They argue that a better technique is to take the order, thank the buyer, and depart as soon as possible. Of course, whether or not to leave the premises immediately depends primarily on your customer. Some purchasers are busy individuals with many pressures and responsibilities, people with little time or inclination for idle gossip after their purchases have been made. Others enjoy an informal conversation or a trip out for a cup of coffee. You should use sensitive judgment in each situation.

How long should you remain with a customer after you've made the sale?

Will You Be Welcomed Back?

After making a sale, you should never depart in such haste that you appear unappreciative of the order. Always be courteous to your customer and anyone else associated with the organization. Whether or not a sale was made, you should express your thanks for *their* time, especially since you want the welcome mat to be out for you the next time you call. Now is not the time to lose control of your emotions because of your disappointment when a prospect turns down your offers. Your post closing activities significantly influence the extent of goodwill created for your company and what sort of a future you may have with the prospect or customer.

A Time for Self–Analysis

As soon as possible after you've left your customer's premises, you should do a **postcall** analysis. This is a careful and objective examination of your sales interview made to help you to improve future sales techniques and customer relations and improve your closing ratio. A useful method for analyzing your sales calls is to ask yourself certain questions, such as those listed in Figure 7.2.

What is the principal purpose of engaging in a postcall analysis?

1. What were my precall objectives?_____
_____

2. Did I achieve these objectives during my sales interview?
   Yes_____ No_____

3. If no, how am I going to alter my activities during the next call?
_____
_____
_____

4. What were some of the weaknesses in my sales presentation and in
   my manner of handling objections?_____
_____
_____
_____

5. Which objections did I handle poorly?_____
_____
_____
_____

6. How might I improve my responses to those objections?_____
_____
_____
_____

7. When should I make a follow-up call?_____

8. What information regarding customer needs or compitition did I
   uncover that should be reported to my management?_____
_____
_____
_____

Figure 7.2 A postcall analysis form.

These are terms that you should now be familiar with:

- close
- buying signals
- body language
- positive-assumption close
- alternate-choice close
- open-question-and-pause close
- multiple-acceptance close
- minor-point close
- contingency close
- future-event close
- special-offer close

- trial-order close
- suggestion close
- counselor close
- last-chance (SRO) close
- summarize-the-benefits close
- direct request close
- by-the-way close
- departure
- buyer's remorse
- postcall analysis

CHAPTER 8

AFTER THE SALE—KEEPING CUSTOMERS SATISFIED

When you finish this chapter, you should be able to:

- Recognize the importance of determining the extent of follow–up necessary for each customer.

- Review the major types of follow–up and customer service activities.

- Identify some of the more common warning signs of deteriorating customer relations.

- Restate the significance of maintaining the goodwill of customers.

CHAPTER 8

We make a living by what we get, but we make a life by what we give.

Winston Churchill
Former British Prime Minister

"Ah..." you smugly say to yourself. "I made the sale, the customer seemed satisfied, my sales manager will be delighted, and most important—*I feel good!* After I return to my white–picketed bungalow tonight, I shall kiss my collie on the tip of her tender nose and then celebrate by carving another notch on the butt of my gold–handled cane, I'll be able to sit back and relax a bit, turn on some soft digitalized *Baroque* music, and then start planning for the next sale."

You ponder for a few moments. "Hmmm, wait just a minute," you think, "Is this really the end—or, instead, merely the beginning? I've only just left the office of my customer, Mr. Herring. In fact, the ink is hardly dry where he signed the purchase order. I'm not in this business to make sales on a 'one–shot basis.' In fact, my earnings and my company's survival are dependent on long–term repeat business. I spent a lot of time with Mr. Herring...didn't even sell him until the third sales call. My company might not even make any money on this concerned with goodwill–building activities or this **post–salescall** period could become a postmortem period instead!"

These hypothetical musings relate directly to the concepts discussed in this chapter. In most instances, the selling process is not complete merely because the customer has stated that he or she will buy your product or service.

Maintaing Customer Satisfaction 8

Closing the Sale

Overcoming Sales Resistance

Presenting and Demonstrating the Sales Message

Approaching Prospective Customers

Finding Qualified Customers (Prospecting)

Figure 8.1 Maintaining customer satisfaction is an important activity in the selling process.

Throughout the entire process, the maintenance of goodwill is important, but it's even more so *after* the purchase or sales call. Regardless of your customer's previous feelings toward your company, your actions at the time of departure and thereafter will significantly influence your long–run success and that of your firm. In the previous chapter, we discussed some of the critical factors associated with customer relations immediately after a sale is closed. Now we examine some important methods for cultivating and maintaining the goodwill of your customers—methods that are part of the follow–up process.

THE FOLLOW–UP

A major life insurance company discloses that in nearly 60 percent of all life insurance lapses, the policy terminates after the second premium payment. The same company points out that after a policyholder makes four premium payments, lapses are negligible. What is the significance of these data? Customers must remain convinced that their buying decisions were correct or repeat purchases are likely to be lost.

Holding onto customers is also important from the standpoint of keeping your company costs down. Studies by Forum Corporation, a Boston–based consulting firm, show that the cost of selling a new customer is five times the cost of retaining that customer once the initial sale is made.[1] You, through the final step in the selling process—the **follow–up**—can influence the satisfaction that your customers derive from their purchases and determine, to a great extent, if they will be repeat customers.

Extent of Follow–up

Assume that there exists in your territory a customer whose purchases have been nominal during the past year—almost the smallest amount bought by any of your accounts—and they are not likely to increase significantly in the future. Also assume that you have a highly profitable account whose purchases amount to nearly 23 percent of the total volume in your territory.

211

What sort of follow–up and service should you provide to each? Naturally the larger, more profitable, account would be entitled to greater attention on your part.

For all customers, you should analyze how extensive your follow–up should be. For most semidormant accounts, an occasional letter or telephone should suffice. For most active customers you might have to make in–person calls every week or two. Customers who have made *or are likely to make* large purchases at some time in the future certainly deserve the utmost in service you can provide.

> *What determines the extent of your follow–up activities with specific customers?*

Don't assume, however, that it is only the larger accounts that demand the most attention. Often a smaller account requires considerable amount of service yet has the potential to be a highly profitable account in the future and, therefore, warrants the investment of your time now. In addition, some larger accounts neither need nor want a lot of contact with their vendors. Marketing expert George W. Wynn, emphasizes such beliefs in the following manner:

"Do not let size alone dictate time spent with a customer. A very large account may not want a lot of attention. One of my *giant* customers accounted for more than 95 percent of a particular product line. The customer told me on the first call, after the business had been secured, to treat his firm like any *good* account, and not to treat it like it amounted to more than 50 percent of my entire sales volume. His statement was made voluntarily, apparently after certain other sales representatives literally 'ran over' my customer."[2]

Many salespeople have noticed that about 80 percent of their customers provide them with about 20 percent of total sales volume in their territories. Conversely, about 80 percent of total sales volume comes from only 20 percent of their customers. So prevalent is the tendency that a concept called the **80/20 rule** is regularly bandied about among sales managers.

Importance of Follow–up

Your principal responsibility as a salesperson is to sell products or services profitably. This should be your rule of reason when servicing accounts. Your time is limited, but time spent with customers is often an investment in greater sales and profits for the future. Even accounts that are semidormant or lacking in potential might become high–volume purchasers if service and follow–up activities can change their attitudes toward you and your company. Furthermore, the follow–up can provide you with excellent opportunities to obtain referrals from your existing customers.

TYPES OF FOLLOW–UP ACTIVITIES

Follow–up activities vary substantially by industry and product. Some categories of customers may require little in the way of attention after the initial sale, while others, such as a retail merchant who buys household products for resale, may require regular assistance with such things as inventory maintenance, merchandise displays, and cooperative advertising programs. Let's look more closely at some of the goodwill–building activities that can be a part of the follow–up.

Maintaining a Good Relationship

You are much more likely to get repeat orders if you develop an amicable relationship with your customers. Any activity that helps to cement this relationship, from a simple "thank you" to hand–delivering a rush order, can benefit both you and your customer. A simple goodwill builder, but one far too frequently overlooked is sending a **thank–you letter** or card soon after a sales card has been made.

Writing thank–you letters should be a routine part of your activities. You can develop a few formats and then modify them to suit each specific customer. The cost of postage and the time expended are minimal compared to the goodwill that letters or cards can create.

213

One company provides its sales representatives with thank–you and congratulations cards for sending to customers. One life insurance agent in Berkeley, California, even sends Thanksgiving Day cards to all of his clients. He says, "My competitors usually send Christmas cards to their clients, so I thought I'd be a bit different." An Arizona agent sends birthday cards to remind policyholders to check the expiration dates of their driving permits, so the birthday card helps to maintain goodwill and keeps the agent's name before the clients. Some salespeople also make a practice of sending get–well cards to their customers. All of these follow–up activities can be summarized by the two words: "Be thoughtful."

What are some ways in which you can show appreciation to your customers?

Remembering the Names of Customers

Have you ever noticed how you tend to feel more friendly toward individuals who use your name during a conversation? Names are important to most people; they are a form of self–identity. As a salesperson, you should especially attempt to remember the names of your customers and use them in conversation. Such activity tends to soften some of the natural sales resistance in many customers.

For most people, remembering names is not automatic; it's a developed art. Study the guidelines in Table 8.1, and you should find that remembering your customers' names is a lot easier in the future.

214

Table 8.1 Guidelines for remembering the names of customers.

When someone is introduced to you:

- Listen carefully to the person's name.

- Repeat the person's name as soon as possible and say the name regularly during the conversation.

- Ask the person how the name is spelled if you are not certain.

- Try to associate the name with something that helps you to remember.

- Develop the practice of greeting your associates by name.

- Don't hesitate to ask people to repeat their names if you forget them.

Why is it important for you to try to remember customers' names?

In–Person Delivery

In some instances, you might be able to develop more satisfied customers by delivering your product in person. For example, life insurance agents frequently deliver policies in person as soon as the contract is prepared and returned from the office. Five major reasons for this type of in–person delivery are:

- To review the features of the policy.

- To reassure the client that a wise purchase was made.

215

- To remind the client when the next premium is due so as to help make the sale stay sold.

- To promote the sale of additional life insurance in the future.

- To solicit referred leads.

Builders and real estate brokers can also make good use of a follow–up after a sale. N. Richard Lewis, president of Lewis & Associates, an advertising and public relations firm, has said:

"There's a double reason for after–sale selling. First, the existing buyer is, and always has been, a great referral source. Second, a builder (or broker) makes friends before he needs them when he keeps selling after he sale. The third–person testimonial to a builder's code of conduct by an existing buyer is an extremely powerful sales tool in today's climate of uncertainty."[3]

What are some advantages of your delivering a product in–person? Is doing so always feasible?

Postpurchase Service and Assistance

Even if the product is not delivered in person, a telephone call or an in person visit may enable you to help your customers with the proper use of your products. Customers who don't know how to use a purchase may blame you or the product for their frustrations and problems. Besides instructing your customers on the "proper care and feeding" of your products, you may also be able to point out additional uses for the items. And sometimes there may be minor repairs or adjustments resulting from faulty installation that you can correct or arrange to have corrected by your service department. In some cases, you may create goodwill just by checking with customers to make certain that their orders were filled and delivered as directed on purchase orders. Table 8.2 offers some specific suggestions regarding follow–up activities.

Table 8.2 Some useful suggestions related to follow–up activities.

- Make a follow–up goodwill–building visit to your customer within a week after delivery of the product to make certain that the order was filled properly.

- Make certain that the product is satisfactory and being used properly.

- Offer suggestions to the customer on ways to make more effective or additional use of the product.

- Use the follow–up visit as an opportunity to obtain new prospects; i.e., ask for referrals.

- Handle any complaints or misunderstandings as soon as possible and with a positive and courteous attitude.

Don't Make "Waste–Time" Calls

When you make in–person follow–up visits, be sure they aren't "waste–time calls." Before making the call, ask yourself, "How is my customer likely to benefit from this call? What do I want to achieve?" Some small talk is acceptable, but remember that the typical customer is under pressure and probably has little interest in merely killing time.

Handling Customer Complaints

No company is perfect, including the one you work for. As a result, complaints are fairly likely to occur, at least occasionally. Follow–ups may be necessary when customers have complaints—whether legitimate or not—about a product or service. Perhaps the order was damaged in shipment, the delivery delayed for some reason, wrong quantities or colors sent, or defective products shipped.

Often you—the salesperson—are the one who will receive the brunt of the complaint and be responsible for resolving such difficulties. Complaints can actually be opportunities in disguise. Rather than being something to dread, a properly handled complaint can serve as a means for the salesperson to cement relations even more firmly. Table 8.3 offers some specific suggestions for handling customer complaints.

How do you treat the customer whose complaint is unfounded?

Table 8.3 Guidelines for handling customer complaints.

- Don't postpone action. Frequently the problem is not as bad as you may have anticipated.,

- Don't be afraid to admit mistakes and to apologize.

- Even when you believe that a complaint is unfounded, show the customer courteous attention and indicate that you will check out the problem.

- Learn to listen to complaints. Often allowing customers to "get it off their chests" lessens the intensity of the gripes.

- Investigate and probe for specific facts. Sometimes there's no valid complaint—the account merely feels irritable.

- Never attack your customers. You will almost always come out on the losing end.

- Don't pass the buck, mark, pound, ruble, or whatever, to your company. When you criticize or blame your company personnel, you are really saying to your customers that you don't have a well-run organization. And don't blame your computers; they, too, are a part of your company. Blaming others in your organization tends to cause your customers to lose confidence in your firm.

Sending Bad–News Messages

Regardless of how good a relationship you've established with customers, there will probably be certain occasions on which you may have to send them unpleasant information, or **bad–news messages**. Can you think of any reasons why you might have to send a customer a bad–news message? Some of the major ones are cited in Table 8.4.

Table 8.4 Principal reasons for sending bad–news messages.

- Refusal of an application (e.g., for credit or insurance).

- A shipping or billing error.

- Unavailability of ordered products.

- Inability to comply with a customer request.

- An unexpected increase in prices.

- A change in company policy that adversely affects the customer.

- A customer complaint.

Probably the single most important suggestion to follow when writing bad news messages is to be empathetic. Carefully reread any letter you intend to send to a customer and ask yourself, "How might I react if this letter were sent to me?" The attitude you convey in such messages goes a long way in influencing future relationships between you and your customers.
A bad–news message should contain at least four elements that we'll refer to in terms of the **BAD–C bad–news technique** to help you remember them. The four letters in the acronym BAD–C stand for:

```
┌─────────────────────┐
│                     │
│     Buffer          │
│                     │
│     Analysis        │
│                     │
│     Decision        │
│                     │
│     Close           │
│                     │
└─────────────────────┘
```

Let's now look briefly at each of these elements.

Buffer. Although you don't want to mislead the reader of your bad–news message, you should attempt to begin your letter with a statement that tends to promote a receptive frame of mind. Remember that the primary goal of any bad–news message should be to convey a fair, reasonable, and concerned attitude in order to maintain positive relations with the customer. The buffer statement, for example could be a simple *expression of thanks* or *appreciation for past orders,* or an *acknowledgment* of some sort, such as for the receipt of a customer's application for credit. It could even be an attempt *to resell* the customer, as in the case where an ordered model was discontinued or out of stock and you attempt to sell a comparable item. Other buffer statements could *compliment* the customer; express an attitude of *cooperation, empathy,* and *understanding;* or reveal certain types of *good news.*

What is the purpose of the buffer portion of a bad–news message?

Analysis. The second segment of a bad–news message expresses why you must do something differently from what the customer might have expected. In some instances—as in routine, confidential, or sensitive matters—stating a reason may be unnecessary or even undesirable. When

221

used, however, the explanation should be presented *before* your actual decision is stated. The explanation should convey a sincere attitude and avoid hackneyed, insincere phrases such as, "We really would like to help you with this matter, but...." Also, avoid using company policy as your scapegoat. Most customers are not placated by the statement, "It's against company policy." Instead, customers usually want to know why—that is, *the reasons*—"it's against policy.

What is wrong with blaming company policy for problems that you may experience with customers?

Decision. Now comes the crucial part of your bad–news message: the decision. Try to convey your decision in a positive manner. Don't tell customers what *you can't do*. For example, if delivery of a purchased product will be two weeks late, your analysis/decision segments of the bad–news message might state something like:

"As you may know, Ms. Treat, the recent trucking strike created some challenges for people in our industry. As a result, your order for ten X–1400s will arrive on your premises no later than November 15 rather than the original November 1 date. We certainly hope that the new date will be acceptable to you."

Try to avoid dogmatic sounding phrases like, "We must refuse...." or "We cannot allow...." Since a bad–news message should also be considered to be a sales message, you might tactfully attempt to resell your customer on the benefits of your products and service.

Which do your customers prefer hearing: What you can do or what you cannot do?

Close. Always attempt to end your message in a positive, sincere, and cordial manner. Your close might include some of the elements cited in Table 8.5.

Table 8.5 Elements that could be included in the close section of a bad–news message.

- An expression of appreciation for past (or possibly future) orders.

- An invitation to offer suggestions, make future purchases, or submit future applications.

- A request to comply with your decision.

- A clear statement of what action, if any, the customer must take to comply with your decision.

- An expression of your continued interest in and appreciation of the customer.

WARNING SIGNS OF DETERIORATING CUSTOMER RELATIONS

You have already read how success in selling is generally the result of repeat sales to satisfied customers. Remember, however, that a customer who seems satisfied today may become disgruntled tomorrow. Just think about the many companies that were once giants but are nonexistent today. Because you work in a competitive world in which there are acceptable substitute sources for nearly every product or service, you should continually be on the lookout for any warning signs that your customers are switching their business to your competitors. See Table 8.6 for a listing of some of the most common warning signs of deteriorating customer relations.

Table 8.6 Common warning signs of deteriorating customer relations

- Changes in purchase volume

- Increased frequency of complaints regarding your products, company, or service

- Repeated comments regarding the merits of competing products or companies

- A less cordial atmosphere during sales calls

- Recently hired personnel who are neither familiar with nor sold on the merits of your products and service

- The absorption of *your customer's organization* by a larger firm

- The absorption of *your organization* by a larger firm

Asking the Customer How Things Are

Knowing how customers feel about your company can enable you to provide and maintain (or correct) the quality of the service expected by most customers. Some firms seem unconcerned or even defensive about the negative attitudes of their customers. More progressive companies, on the other hand, are exceedingly concerned. They realize that the replacement of customers is expensive. Some firms send detailed questionnaires to their accounts as a means of keeping on top of customer attitudes. In order to properly serve your customers, you must understand what your customers' expectations are related to service and quality.

224

The Not–So–Hidden Costs of Customer Alienation

Maintaining a positive relationship with your customers is critical and will help you in achieving your own and your company's goals. On the other hand, we've noted that it usually costs substantially more to obtain new customers than to service existing ones. There are numerous other costs that are also associated with having disgruntled customers.

For example, the customer who has had good reason to develop negative attitudes toward your company is less likely to cooperate during situations that are beyond your control, as during strikes and resource shortages. The dissatisfied customer is likely to be far less accepting of even trivial problems, thus increasing the time that you—the salesperson—will have to spend trying to get things back to normal.

Disenchanted customers also may begin to generalize negatively about a variety of things associated with your company. For example, if customers feel that service is poor, they may begin to wonder whether production quality standards might not also be poor. Furthermore, unhappy customers are less apt to want to increase their volume of purchases, since they might feel that to do so will only amplify the unpleasantness of their dealings with your company.

THE IMPORTANCE OF GOODWILL

Goodwill is a factor related to customer attitude and sentiments toward you and your company. The loss of customer goodwill is, in effect, the loss of sales. Goodwill building is not automatic. It requires a deliberate, conscientious, and sincere concern about customer interests and needs over extended periods of time. Virtually every step in the selling process has an influence on goodwill.

Goodwill is not concrete—you can't put your finger on it or measure it accurately in terms of dollars. Nevertheless, goodwill is of significant value since it helps the salesperson in making initial and repeat sales. Furthermore, customers with favorable attitudes toward your company and its products are also excellent sources of referral business.

225

THE IMPORTANCE OF ETHICAL BEHAVIOR

What does the word **ethics** mean to you? It is a term that is probably easier to define than to illustrate. *Ethics* deals with *standards of conduct or morals established by the current and past attitudes, moods, and practices of a particular society.* Business ethics, in simple terms, relates to standards of "right" and "wrong" conduct in business relationships. A factor complicating the concept of ethics is that what is considered "wrong" by one person, firm, industry, or country may be considered "right" or even desirable, by another.

Changing Standards of Ethics

It's not easy, therefore, to determine in absolute terms what constitutes ethical behavior. The problem is further complicated by changing standards. Practices once considered unethical have later been accepted and, therefore, have become ethical. Here's an example of changing standards. Prior to the 1980s, debates raged as to whether advertising by doctors, dentists, pharmacists, and lawyers should have been considered a breach of professional ethics. Today, however, advertisements by "legal advisers" and other professionals are relatively commonplace. A more current example relates to the "rightness" or "wrongness" of American companies paying foreign government officials "consulting fees" for assistance in obtaining sales in other countries. Based on American standards of ethics, such payments constitute bribes. However, in some other cultures such payments are considered acceptable practice and even necessary to obtain business.

Legal Versus Moral Standards

There is a significant difference between *legal* standards and *ethical* standards. The former can be enforced by statute, while the latter are determined by custom and attitudes. Many *unethical* practices are also *illegal,* but can you think of an activity that's *legal* but considered *unethical?* Here's one example: selling a product that meets legal standards but is borderline with regard to consumer safety. Another example could be selling a product or service that a customer can't use. Falling into the first

226

category were the three wheel all–terrain vehicles (ATVs), which killed an estimated 900 people over a five–year period and injured people at a rate of nearly 1,000 per month. ATVs were legal until 1988 when the Justice Department, backed by the Consumer Product Safety Commission, outlawed their further sales

In general, a good measure of whether or not a business practice is unethical is found in the answers to two questions:

- Is the activity contrary to current acceptable legal and moral practices?

- Is the activity likely to be injurious to others?

Affirmative responses to these questions could mean disaster for some firms.

Responsibilities toward Your Customers

As a salesperson, one of your major responsibilities is to serve your customers. The types of salespeople we have been concerned with in this text are professionals, honest and sincere individuals who are genuinely concerned with serving and assisting customers with their problems and needs and who follow through promptly on complaints and service needs. The kind of salespeople in demand among today's marketing organizations are not the con artists but rather individuals who can readily adapt their style and approach to fit the characteristics and needs of their customers. Getting the order is only the beginning for the creative, professional salesperson. Repeat orders, which significantly influence the survival of most companies, are directly dependent on the goodwill established by the salesperson.

227

As a salesperson who is aware of all this, you are likely to find yourself facing innumerable pressures and temptations in relation to your customers. You will get far more satisfaction from your job over the long run—and be more likely to keep it—if you following generally acceptable ethical practices in all your dealings.

NOT THE END...ONLY THE BEGINNING!

You now have come to the end of this guidebook intended to assist you in honing your selling skills. However, this shouldn't be the end of your studying. Take the time to read regularly. Developing sloppy or lazy patterns is not particularly difficult, and we all need reminders from time to time on how we should be behaving in our daily activities. Furthermore, you can expect to have occasional ups and downs in your moods in your selling career. During such periods, reread sections of this book, which could help to recharge those weakening batteries of yours. And remind yourself that everyone has such fluctuating moods. You will come out of them if you attempt to maintain a positive attitude. So work hard, be optimistic, focus on your prospect's needs, practice! practice! practice!, and you find that you, too, will *Improve Your Selling Effectiveness!*

These are terms that you should now be familiar with:

- post–sales–call period
- bad–news messages
- follow up
- BAD–C bad–news technique
- 80/20 rule
- goodwill
- thank–you letter
- ethics

NOTES

1. Patricia Sellers, "Getting Customers To Love You," *Fortune,* March 13, 1989, pp. 6–33.

2. Related to the author during a review of an earlier edition of a book.

3. "Powerful Sales Tool Neglected," *Oakland Tribune,* May 5, 1975, pp. 1C, 4C.

4. "Outlawing a Three–Wheeler," *Time International Edition,* January 11, 1988, P. 39.

GLOSSARY

acknowledging: An effort by the salesperson to show the prospect that the salesperson understands and sympathizes with the prospect's feelings of resistance (6).

actual self: The way we *really* see ourselves in relation to our environment (1).

advantages: Factors inherent in a product or service that may provide benefits to a prospective customer (4).

agreeing and neutralizing: The effort by the salesperson to "disarm" the prospect by appearing to recognize the merits of the prospect's objections before returning to the sales message with renewed vigor (6).

AIDCA concept: AIDCA is an acronym that symbolizes five steps or stages that a prospect's mind goes through, with assistance from a salesperson, on the way to making a buying decision; the steps are Attention, Interest, Desire, Conviction, and Action (4).

alternate-choice close: A closing technique in which the salesperson provides the prospect with a choice between two positive alternatives (1).

approach: The step in the selling process intended to gain the prospective customer's attention for the purpose of arousing interest and desire in the product and salesperson's message (3).

Asch conformity studies: Research by Solomon E: Asch that showed the effect of group pressure on the perception and attitudes of individual members of a group (1).

aspirational reference group: Groups an individual is not a member of but would like to belong to (1).

attitude: The belief and feelings individuals have that influence the ways they behave toward other people, objects, and ideas (1).

231

audiovisual presentation: An automated type of sales presentation that makes use of various kinds of equipment to relate product features and advantages to customer benefits; usually requires a salesperson to answer additional questions and to close the sale (4).

BAD-C bad-news technique: An acronym that symbolizes the four major elements of bad-news messages, which are *B*uffer, *A*nalysis, *D*ecision, and *C*lose (8).

bad-news messages: As applied to customer relations, messages, often in letter form, to customers expressing unpleasant information in a manner that does not cause a deterioration of customer goodwill (8):

benefits: In selling, a product characteristic that can prove useful or profitable to a prospective customer (4):

blind referral: An approach technique that makes vague, rather than specific, reference to third parties as a means of arousing prospect interest in the salesperson's message and products (3).

blitz technique: A prospecting method intended to saturate a particular region or group in a short period of time (2):

body language: A form of nonverbal communication in which body movements convey meaning (7):

buyer's remorse: The feelings of doubt or regret that some customers develop shortly after making an affirmative buying decision (7):

buying center: A concept, rather than a formal group or place, that represents all of the people who either directly or indirectly influence purchases (3):

buying committees: Ongoing, established groups whose functions is to determine the best sources for their organizational purchases (1, 2, 3):

buying motives: Factors that cause or drive people to purchase particular products (1):

232

buying signals: Expressions, either physical or verbal, of a prospect's desire to make a buying decision (3, 6):

by-the-way close: A closing technique in which the salesperson appears to have given up and then attempts one more close; tends to relax the prospect's defenses (7):

centers of influence: Individuals who are well known in a community and who may serve as sources of prospective customers (2).

civic and social groups: Organizations whose members can be excellent sources of prospective customers (2).

close (closing): The attempt by the salesperson to motivate the prospective customer into making an affirmative decision regarding the purchase of a product or service (3, 6).

clubs: Social groups whose members can be excellent sources of prospects (2).

cognitive dissonance: A form of stress caused by uncertainty as to whether a purchase should have been made at a particular time (1).

cold calls: Calling on prospects who have not been contacted previously (2).

cold canvas approach: An approach to prospecting that involves contacting as many individuals as possible in a particular group or area; frequently used by door-to-door salespeople (2): *complimenting-customers approach:* An approach technique that extends to customers sincere flattery related to achievements or events that have affected the customers or their firms (3): *contingency close:* A closing technique in which the salesperson agrees to do something provided the prospect agrees to make a purchase (7).

converting (boomerang): The sales activity of converting objections into reasons for buying a product or service (6): *counselor close:* A closing technique in which the salesperson advises the customer how and what to buy (7).

culture: The environmental influences handed down from one generation to another (1).

curiosity-appeal approach: An approach technique that attempts to arouse a prospective customer's interest by appealing to his or her natural curiosity (3).

customer-benefit approach: An approach technique that uses statements or questions for the purpose of enabling prospects to see how they can benefit from the purchase of a product or service (3).

custom production: Products that are produced to satisfy the specific needs of a particular customer rather than customers in general (1):

cyclical demand: Demand for a product that tends to fluctuate widely depending on economic conditions, inventory, policies, and buyer expectations (1).

demonstration: The act of actually displaying and showing the use of a product as visual proof of sales claims (5).

denying: The act of refuting an untrue accusation made by a prospect toward the salesperson or company; must be used with caution (6).

departure: The various activities associated with making a smooth exit from the customer's premises (7).

derived demand: Demand for a product or resource, such as silicon chips, that results from demand for another product, such as computers (1).

direct request close: A closing technique in which the salesperson simply asks the prospect for the order (7): *dramatizing:* Related to sales presentations, efforts by the salesperson to use product demonstration techniques that tend to stir a prospect's imagination or emotions (5).

80/20 rule: A concept based on the experience of many sales managers indicating that about 80 percent of their customers are responsible for only about 20 percent of total sales volume: Therefore, about 80 percent of their sales volume comes from only about 20 percent of their customers (8).

endless-chain method: The activity of obtaining names of prospective customers from existing customers (2).

ethics: The standards of conduct or morals established by the current and past attitudes, moods, and practices of a particular society (8).

features: The prominent parts or characteristics that can help to sell a product when they are related to product benefits and customer needs (4).

follow up: The types of sales and service activities that follow the sales call; activities that tend to assist customers and foster favorable customer attitudes toward you, your company, and its products (8).

forestalling: An effort by a salesperson to anticipate specific objections and answer them before they arise (6).

free-service approach: An approach technique that offers something free for the purpose of showing interest in the customer and arousing his or her interest: (3).

FUN-FAB OPTIC concept: An acronym symbolizing the essential ingredients of most sales presentations, stresses the importance of First Uncovering Needs, relating the Features, Advantages, and benefits of the product to the customer's needs, and the elements of handling Objections, Proving, Trial closing, Insuring, and Closing (4).

future-event close: A closing technique in which the salesperson attempts to motivate the prospect to buy now in order to avoid the greater future losses that would result if the purchase were postponed (7).

gatekeeper: An individual, or individuals, in a "buying center" who creates obstacles to the making of a sale by a salesperson (3).

goodwill: An intangible factor related to the attitudes that customers hold toward a company and its products; an essential factor in maintaining customers over time (8).

guiding: The sales activity of supporting favorable comments made by the prospect toward the product in order to move the prospect away from focusing on negative feelings (6).

hierarchy of needs: A theory developed by Abraham Maslow that refers to the arrangement of person's needs in order of priority (1).

high involvement products: More expensive products that are infrequently purchased and require more consumer information prior to purchase (1).

ideal self: The way we want to be seen or *would like* to view ourselves (1).

ignoring: A technique for handling objections that simply sidesteps a prospect's objections when they appear flimsy and without merit; should be used with caution (6).

insuring: An element in a sales presentation that offers information intended to reassure the prospect that minimal risk will result from his or her purchasing the product (4).

last-chance (SRO) close: A closing technique in which the salesperson suggests the importance of buying now to avoid disappointment later (7).

listening: An important activity that enables salespeople to uncover needs, discover reasons for buyer resistance, and calm down excessively emotional customers.(6).

low involvement products: Lower-priced products that are routinely bought without a lot of analysis (1).

market concentration: A characteristic of the marketplace when large numbers of customers are situated within a relatively small geographical area (1).

minor-point close: A closing technique in which the salesperson attempts to obtain agreement on a minor point so as to check the receptiveness of a prospect (7).

mirroring: The act of restating to the prospect what the salesperson thinks the prospect has just said; allows prospects to reconsider their own words.(6).

motive: A feeling or condition that leads to specific activity intended to bring about satisfaction (1)

multiple-acceptance close: A closing technique in which the salesperson obtains a series of agreements leading to a final close (7).

multiple buying decisions: Decisions as to whether or not to purchase that are made by more than one person, such as in the case of buying committees or buying centers (1, 3).

multiple-sense appeals: Factors in a sales presentation that tend to appeal to more than one of the prospect's senses (5).

needs: The condition of deprivation, occurs when something, such as food, is missing from a person's environment (1, 4).

negative reference groups: Groups that a person doesn't want to identify with, so that he or she adopts attitudes opposed to them (1).

objections: Resistance by a prospective customer toward various aspects of a salesperson's sales presentation (3, 5).

"OK-names" approach: An approach technique that attempts to gain attention by offering prospective customers the names of well-known users of the salesperson's products or services (3).

open-question-and-pause close: A closing technique in which the salesperson asks a question that can't be answered with a simple yes or no and then waits for the prospect to answer (7).

outlined presentation: An organized sales presentation that follows a predetermined checklist of major points to be covered (4).

participational reference group: A group that individuals are integral members of, such as their families, clusters of friends, and their neighbors; buying habits are often derived from reference groups (1).

party groups: Gathering of relatively large numbers of prospective customers, typically in the home of host persons who have invited them to sales demonstrations of certain products such as cosmetics and household wares (2).

patronage motives: The reason why people repeatedly and consistently buy from a particular firm (1).

perception: An activity or skill related to seeing things as they really are rather than as we expect (1).

peer effect: The influence our associates have on what we see, think, and do (1).

positive-assumption close: A closing technique in which the salesperson assumes that the prospect wants to make a purchase and will act accordingly (7).

post-sales-call period: A critical period that follows the sales interview; sales and service activities during this period significantly influence future customer relationships and goodwill (8).

postcall analysis: A form completed after a sales call by the salesperson for the purpose of recording and analyzing the nature of the discussion, what customer needs were uncovered, what objections were raised, and future plans for a follow-up sales call (7).

postponing: The intentional delaying by a salesperson of a response to an objection until ample sales information has been presented to the prospect (6).

preapproach: The sales activity that involves obtaining as much relevant information as necessary about prospects before contacting them personally (2).

primary needs: Factors that are vital to human survival, such as oxygen, food, clothing, shelter, sleep, and so on; also termed *physical* needs (1).

problem-solving approach: An approach technique that emphasizes how the purchase of a particular good or service can create solutions to specific customer problems (3).

product approach: An approach technique that uses the product itself or various visual aids as a means of arousing a potential customer's interest in the salesperson's message and products (3).

programmed presentation (survey): A sales presentation that attempts during the first visit to examine and analyze a prospect's problems and needs: Typically, a follow-up sales call is then required to offer a combined written and oral presentation (4).

projection: The tendency to attribute to others some of our own values and motives (1).

prospecting: The step in the selling process that involves locating potential customers: (2).

prospects: Persons or organizations who qualify, have buying authority, and can benefit from the purchase of a particular good or service (2).

proving: The sales activity of using available evidence to substantiate the benefit claims made by the salesperson (4).

purchase decision process: The stages that most purchasers are believed to go through when trying to decide whether to make a purchase (1).

qualifying prospects: The activity of obtaining the information necessary to determine whether a lead or suspect is likely to be a good prospect (2).

questioning: When used as a technique to handle objections, the effort to move a prospect's objections from the general to the specific so that the salesperson can understand and deal more effectively with them (6).

questioning approach: A technique of approaching customers that helps to maintain interest even when an answer is not expected; can be used to uncover needs of prospective customers (3).

rational buying motives: Reasons for purchasing goods or services from its own customers (1).

reference groups: Groups that we tend to identify with and derive many of our attitudes from (1).

referral approach: An approach technique that makes use of the names of or letters of introduction from personal acquaintances of the prospective customer as a means of gaining his or her attention (3).

referral method: The activity of obtaining a personal note or letter of introduction from existing customers along with names of prospective customers (2).

role playing: An activity that involves creating a realistic situation and then acting out the various parts; frequently used in sales training (6).

sales aids: Items used to help dramatize a sales presentation and appeal to the buying motives of prospects (5).

sales presentation: A message given by a salesperson to a prospective customer for the purpose of arousing a feeling of need and showing how the product can satisfy this recognized need (4).

sales associates: Individuals who don't work for the same firm as the salesperson but who are in the position to provide leads to the salesperson (2).

sample/gift approach: An approach technique that offers free samples or gifts for the purpose of arousing the prospective customer's interest in the salesperson's message and products (3).

secondary needs: Factors of a social or psychological nature that tend to motivate people, such as the needs to feel secure, to be with people, to be respected, and to have feelings of accomplishment (1).

selective perception: The tendency for people to see or hear only what they want or are set to see and hear and to tune out much of the rest of a given situation (1).

self-concept (self image): The way we view ourselves and the way we feel others view us (1).

selling process: The essential elements involved in the activity of personal selling: includes prospecting, the approach, the presentation, demonstration, overcoming sales resistance the close, and keeping customers satisfied (2).

showmanship approach: An approach technique that presents product features in a dramatic fashion for the purpose of gaining a prospective customer's attention and interest in a product or service (3).

showmanship: The act of vividly and dramatically demonstrating the features, advantages, and benefits of a product or service in unusual ways to acquire and maintain the prospect's attention and interest; should have multiple-sense appeals where possible (5).

situational selling: The process of drawing on past sales experiences and knowledge when confronting a prospective buyer while also recognizing that each selling situation and customer are somewhat unique and may require a flexible and distinct presentation (4).

situational demonstration: The recognition that each prospective customer is unique and that the type of demonstration used should be one that appeals to the particular prospect (5).

snap judgments: The tendency to form hastily conceived first impressions of people and things (1).

social class: A group of people who have similar status in society, generally determined by attained educational levels, occupations, and locations of residence (1).

special-offer close: A closing technique in which the salesperson provides the prospect with an added inducement, such as a discount (7).

spotters: Employees of a company whose responsibility is to locate leads for more experienced salespeople (2).

standard memorized presentation (canned): A highly structured or "canned" sales presentation in which the salesperson expresses a predetermined message (4).

suggestion close: A closing technique in which the salesperson relates to a previous point that suggested a purchase should be made (7).

summarize-the-benefits close: A closing technique in which the salesperson attempts, by blending a summary of the benefits with one of the other closing techniques, to guide the prospect into making a positive buying decision (7).

surprise approach: An approach technique that utilizes the element of nonexpectation as a means of gaining the prospective customer's attention (3).

surveys: A prospecting technique that involves the use of questionnaires to uncover potential needs of prospective customers (2).

suspects (leads): People or organizations that could be buyers of a good or service but have not yet been qualified as definite prospects: (2).

team selling: A sales situation in which two or more salespeople make a sales presentation to a potential customer (1).

telemarketing: A broad set of activities that involves the use of the telephone to support and, at times, to substitute for personal face-to-face selling; frequently used in prospecting activities (2).

telephone and mail inquiries: A source of prospects that develops when prospective customers telephone or write for additional product information (2).

testimonial letter: A written document indicating that a customer has been pleased with a salesperson and his or her company's products and service; such a letter may be an aid in prospecting and in approaching prospective customers (2).

thank-you letter: A goodwill-building item that expresses to customers or prospects a salesperson's appreciation for having been granted a sales interview or having received an order (8).

3F's method: A technique for handling objections that attempts to "disarm" the prospect by appearing to understand how the prospect *feels,* pointing out that others have *felt* similarly in the past, and showing what people *found* after trying the product (6).

tickler files: A system designed to remind a salesperson when to make follow-up calls on and what to discuss with prospective customers (2).

T.O. method: The activity of *turning over* a difficult customer to another salesperson (6).

trade fairs/exhibitions: Displays of manufacturers' products at gatherings of prospective customers (2).

trial closing: An effort by a salesperson, made at any time during a sales presentation, to obtain an affirmative buying decision from the prospect: (4).

trial-order close: A closing technique in which the salesperson attempts to get the prospect to test the product on a limited scale (7).

useful-idea approach: An approach that attempts to gain a prospective customer's attention by offering helpful ideas (3).

video cassettes/computer diskettes: Software materials that can display advertising on television or computer screens to spark consumer interest; such materials when requested by mail can furnish prospecting leads to salespeople (2).

visual aids: Items that can be used in sales presentations to appeal to a prospect's sense of sight, such as flip charts, graphs, and portfolios (5).

weighing: A technique for handling objections that shows a prospect how advantages of a product outweigh disadvantages; often makes use of a "T-account" by listing advantages on one side and disadvantages on the other (6).